The
Mechanics
of
Athletics

GEOFFREY H. G. DYSON

Director of Physical Education,
Winchester College

Chief National Coach,
Amateur Athletic Association (1947-1961)

UNIVERSITY OF LONDON PRESS LTD

ISBN 0 340 17442 0

First published 1962
Sixth edition copyright © 1973 G. H. G. Dyson

University of London Press Ltd
St Paul's House, Warwick Lane, London EC4P 4AH
Illustrations by D. R. Dimmock
Printed and bound in England
by Hazell Watson & Viney Ltd, Aylesbury, Bucks

This book is due for return on or before the last date shown below.

Preface to the Sixth Edition

In suggesting the direction in which the truths of the mechanics of athletics may lie—what is probable, how theories on this subject hang together and what follows if they be admitted—the writer has again found it necessary to correct, modify and expand his text in a new edition.

In particular, the chapter on Pole Vaulting has been re-written, and several illustrations and an Appendix describing some turntable experiments have been added.

Anyone working in such a field as this must necessarily check with those whose opinions he values. I am therefore grateful to my friend, Mr. B. J. Hopper, M.Sc., whom I have consulted; my debt to him will be clear from the references in footnotes. My thanks are also due to Dr James E. Counsilman for permission to quote from his book, *The Science of Swimming*.

Winchester   G.H.G.D.
February 1973

Acknowledgments

The mechanics of track and field athletics have been a special interest of mine for more than twenty-five years, and I welcome this opportunity to express gratitude to the many who, through writing, lecturing or discussion, have taught me most of what I have learned.

In particular, I am indebted to three friends. First, Mr. C. Arrowsmith, B.Sc., A.M.I.Mech.E., now Deputy Head of the Department of Mechanical Engineering, Loughborough College of Technology, whose patient, clear explanation helped me in the beginning. Second, Mr. A. D. Munrow, B.Sc., Director of Physical Education in the University of Birmingham, a constant source of advice and encouragement. And third, Mr. E. F. Housden, O.B.E., M.C., M.A., to whom I am especially beholden for generous and invaluable comment in the preparation of this book.

LONDON
April 1962

G. H. G. D.

Contents

Contents

PART II

Introduction

An important feature in the development of British track and field athletics coaching has been the spreading of a knowledge of the mechanical principles essential to its skills. For human motion, with its boundless variability, obeys the laws of all motion; and athletic skill at the highest level always applies these same principles to the utmost advantage.

The scientifically-minded youth of today are ready to accept the truths of mechanics and, certainly, the subject as applied to sport is of considerable interest to young people, especially boys. In the classroom it can be used to relate physics to physical education, for athletic examples are more 'alive' and meaningful than many normally used in the physics lesson.

However, in the teaching of skill on the sports ground, in the gymnasium or in the swimming pool mechanical explanation should be used with discretion, for athletes differ widely in intelligence, education and interests; while some will be intellectually stimulated and athletically improved by it, others will be confused.

Because athletes learn their skills through their kinaesthetic sensations, translating what they see or what they are told in terms of 'what it feels like' to do, more descriptive (if mechanically inaccurate) language is often preferable to the jargon of mechanics. Herein lies the art, as opposed to the science, of coaching athletics.

Again, the value of this kind of explanation to the performer varies from event to event. For example, the mechanics of running are extraordinarily complex, yet most good middle and long-distance runners develop an efficient style without giving the matter much thought. On the other hand, sprinters, hurdlers and field event athletes need a more technical, analytical approach to the mastering of skill.

Speaking generally, all athletes are best left unaware of the exact nature of their movements and need only sufficient detail to correct faults, satisfy curiosity and inspire confidence.

The Mechanics of Athletics

With teachers and coaches, however, a knowledge of mechanics is an essential tool with which to distinguish between important and unimportant, correct and incorrect, cause and effect, possible and impossible. With such knowledge they can observe and deduce much more than otherwise from athletic performance; and whereas the many skills of track and field are all too-frequently viewed as a clutter of isolated experiences, each with its quite separate picture and puzzle, through a knowledge of mechanics teachers and coaches can recognise and explore likenesses, seeing what is general in what is particular, and so create a unity. It can also help towards a better understanding of other subjects, e.g. weight training, which count in the training of the athlete.

The mechanics of athletics is a comparatively undeveloped field in which, because of a multiplicity of unknown or only partially known factors, precise calculation is often impossible; here, too, principles applicable to rigid bodies are being applied to bodies that are far from rigid.

Athletes differ in their masses, skeletal formations, leverages and flexibilities; the magnitude, direction and effectiveness of their various body forces are often difficult or impossible to determine exactly; and accuracy has sometimes to be sacrificed in order to reduce the irregular human shape to more convenient geometric forms.

Even so, such deductions and rough estimates can be of sufficient accuracy to be of real practical value to the athletics coach or teacher —but they must be the result of careful observation and unbiased interpretation, and allowance must be made for laws other than mechanical ones (e.g. biological laws) which also play a part in the analysis of human motion.

It is hoped, therefore, that this book, although lacking in theoretical perfection, will yet achieve something of practical significance. Its contents are based upon the estimated needs of coaches of track and field athletics and physical educators. It assumes no previous knowledge of mechanics, yet it is hoped also to interest the expert.

Part 1 deals with matters of fact. It attempts to define relevant fundamental mechanical principles, taking many examples from familiar sporting experiences. Deliberately, its content arrangement does not conform to that of the normal mechanics textbook. Also deliberate is the avoidance of formulae wherever possible, as these are not always essential to clear explanation, and people untrained in mathematics are often confused by them. But, in the absence of formulae, words carry an extra burden and must be read carefully for their full meaning.

Introduction

The writer has assumed that most readers are still better able to think in feet and pounds, rather than metres and kilogrammes, and that, therefore, the use here of the less familiar M.K.S. units (metre, kilogramme, second) would constitute just another barrier to understanding. For those wishing to use metric units, however, the required conversion numbers are 9·8 m for 32 ft and 1 kilogramme for 2·2 lb.

Part II, in which the techniques of the various track and field events are analysed, is less factual—for we have so much more to learn. Here, often, the thesis is mere speculation—a hypothesis to be tested and discussed against further lines of research.

It must be emphasised that an analysis of mechanical principles is but one aspect of the examination of athletic performance. In our quest for the complete picture we must seek the help of other sciences which arrive at somewhat different conceptions, for they can deduce only those facts obtainable through their special methods.

Thus, to the physiologist, athletic performance is a phenomenon of cells, humours, tissues and nutrient fluids obeying organic laws. The psychologist sees the athlete as a consciousness and a personality, while, to the physicist, he suggests a machine unique in its organisation, adaptiveness and complexity.

To the imaginative student of athletics, the borders of the various specialities are seen to overlap; the techniques of one science become meaningful and illuminating in others.

Motion*

All motion in track and field athletics, whether of an athlete's whole body, a part of it, or the movement of some object of athletic apparatus (like a pole or shot) behaves in accordance with certain well-established principles, and is subject to the same mechanical laws† as everything else on earth, animate and inanimate. Motion is of two kinds, linear and angular.

Linear (often referred to as **translatory**) **motion** is characterised by the progression of a body in a straight line, with all its parts moving the same distance, in the same direction and at the same speed. One seldom sees pure linear motion in track and field events, but it is a factor to be taken into account, none the less. Fig. 1 gives an example of it in another sport, tobogganing. However, in so far as a sprinter's movements in a

Figure 1

Figure 2

100 yards race can be thought of as being in a straight line, from start to finish (i.e. ignoring the rotational movements of arms, legs and trunk), linear movement *is* apparent, and there are many other such examples in athletics.

* The modern theory of motion was largely the creation of Galileo Galilei; and the century following his death in 1642 saw the establishment of the principles of Motion (the work of several great minds) along lines initiated by him.

† The branch of mechanics which deals specifically with motion resulting from the action of force is called *dynamics*; that branch which deals with a study of balanced forces is called *statics*.

Angular motion is far more common in all human and animal loco-motion because, mechanically speaking, such motion is dependent upon a system of levers of which they are constructed. It is of such importance in track and field athletics that a special chapter is devoted to it later in this book (pages 64–119).

Meanwhile, the chief difference between angular and linear motion is that whereas in angular movement one part of the object—the axis—remains fixed in relation to the others (as, for example, when the arm rotates about the shoulder joint (Fig. 2) or a discus rotates in the air (Fig. 3)), in linear motion every particle of the object travels the same distance simultaneously, moving from one location to another.

Figure 3   *Figure 4*

A body can perform linear and angular movements simultaneously: when, during its rotations or angular displacements, its axis moves along a certain path. The motion of a rolling wheel (Fig. 4) is an example of this. The wheel's hub moves in a linear fashion because of the rotations of the rim: an example of the many objects, including animals and human beings, which move *as a whole* in a straight path as a result of rotational movement of some part. A sprinter obtains linear movement through the rotary action of his feet; in throwing or putting, the rotational movements of an athlete's body can be co-ordinated to impart linear motion to the missile.

In all athletic activities the best results call for a blending of linear and rotational motion; the sprinter's rotational foot movements must be co-ordinated with the linear vertical motion of his whole body; similarly, the hammer-thrower's forward movement across the circle must be co-ordinated with his turns.

Uniform and non-uniform motion

The motion of a body is said to be *uniform* when equal distances are covered in equal times. It is *non-uniform* when unequal distances are covered in equal times. Thus, a 4 min 16 sec miler running at a perfectly even pace would run with uniform motion (i.e. 16 sec per 110 yards); but a sprinter with intermediate times of 5.3 sec (50 yds), 6·2 sec (60 yds), 7·0 sec (70 yds), 8·0 sec (80 yds), and 10·2 sec (100 yds) would be travelling with non-uniform motion.

The sprinter's motion from 60 to 70 yards would be described as *accelerated* as he covers the 10 yards distance 0·1 sec faster than the 10 yards immediately preceding (i.e. 50 to 60) and as he loses speed from the 70 yards mark his motion from then on is *retarded*. These are both loose analogies, since the process of taking even a single running stride can involve acceleration and retardation.

Velocity

In mechanics a distinction is made between velocity and speed, although, in track and field athletics, for most purposes the terms are synonymous and, for the athlete, the term 'speed' is more meaningful than 'velocity'. *Velocity* includes the *direction* of travel as well as the *rate*. A runner may move at a speed of 24 m.p.h., but to state his velocity we must find in which direction he is travelling; he may have a velocity of 24 m.p.h. due north.

The rate of motion or the speed of an object is given in units of length and time. Thus a speed of 24 m.p.h. may also be stated as 35·2 ft per second.

Possessing *magnitude* and *direction*, velocity is a *vector quantity* and can therefore be represented diagrammatically by straight lines (pages 18–20).

Acceleration

Very rarely in athletics are velocities constant; more often they change in their amount or direction, or both at once. As we have seen, when the velocity of an object (e.g. an athlete or a missile) changes in amount it is said to be *retarded* (if it continually decreases) or *accelerated* (if the velocity continually increases).

But the term *acceleration* is used in mechanics in either the gaining or losing of speed. Whenever the acceleration of an object is opposite in direction to its velocity (as when our sprinter lost velocity after reaching 70 yards) the term *negative acceleration* is used, and when acceleration and velocity are in the same direction (as when the sprinter picks up speed initially) the acceleration is called *positive*.

By 'acceleration', therefore is meant *the rate of change of velocity*.

The following is an example of positive acceleration: let us suppose

14

that an athlete running at a rate of 22 ft per second (i.e. 15 m.p.h.) increases his speed so that it reaches 33 ft per second (i.e. 22½ m.p.h.) in 5 sec. His change in speed is 33 minus 22, or 11 ft per second. But this is not his acceleration; it is only the change in velocity.

The change in velocity, 11 ft per second, occurred in 5 sec, so the change in velocity *per second* is 11 ft per second divided by 5, or 2⅕ ft per second every second. Each second the velocity increased 2⅕ ft per second. The acceleration—the 'pick-up', to use sprinting parlance— was therefore 2⅕ ft per second per second.

Thus every statement of acceleration must contain two units of time: one for velocity and one for the time during which that change in velocity occurred.

What has been said concerns *uniform acceleration*, but in athletics acceleration is often of a non-uniform character. However, we can only calculate the true value of an acceleration at any instant by taking as a basis the increase of velocity during a period of time, making the latter as small as possible.

Being a vector quantity, acceleration has *direction* as well as magnitude; a runner taking a bend (Fig. 37), for example, is accelerating even if his speed is constant—because of his continuous change in velocity towards the inside of the bend at right angles to his running direction. Likewise, a hammer rotating at uniform speed has an acceleration towards its axis. (See page 46 and pages 209–16.)

Motion of freely falling bodies

As performance in every athletic activity is influenced by the force of gravity, the laws of freely falling bodies apply to all track and field events. Strictly speaking, these laws are applicable only to motion in air-free space, but in athletics for all practical purposes air resistance in falling can be ignored, as can the decrease in acceleration with altitude (see page 48).

The actions of the efficient runner reduce to a minimum the dropping of body weight on each stride and, therefore, the degree of upward movement which would otherwise be wasted on raising it again. The good hurdler takes his obstacles with little to spare in order to return to ground quickly. The high-jumper trains to improve both the power and direction of his take-off drive to gain more height, 'defying' gravity. Again, the time during which shots, javelins, hammers and discoi are in flight is largely governed by these same laws.

For a hundred and more centuries, between the earliest civilised man

15

and the time of Galileo, it was believed that heavier things fall faster in proportion to their weight. However, two bodies let fall simultaneously side by side (starting from rest) fall equally quickly, regardless of weight, size or their material. If they are cemented together to form one body this in no way alters the distance fallen in a given period; in fact, a heavy athlete falls no quicker than a light one. And this is so whether or not the fall is directly downward. (See also page 48.)

The vertical velocity of a freely falling object increases by 32 ft* per second every second (Fig 5*a*), and in rising it loses vertical velocity at the same rate. The distance it falls is proportional to the square of the time—i.e. in one unit of time, 1; in two units, 4; in three units, 9 and so on—and can be calculated from the formula $d = \frac{1}{2}gt^2$, where *d* is the distance of rise or fall (vertically) measured in feet, $g = 32$ and $t = $ the time in seconds. In analysing athletic movement it is sometimes useful to know, for example, than an object drops 1 ft in $\frac{1}{4}$ sec.; 4 ft in $\frac{1}{2}$ sec; 9 ft in $\frac{3}{4}$ sec; and 16 ft in 1 sec (Fig. 5 *b*).

An object falling for three seconds will, therefore, drop 144 ft (i.e. 16 ft × 9), will have a final speed of 32 × 3 or 96 ft per sec, and its average speed will be half of this, i.e. 48 ft per sec. The distance it falls in this time will be the average speed multiplied by the time of falling, i.e. 48 × 3 or 144 ft. Released vertically with an initial upward speed of 96 ft per sec from a point 144 ft below its original level, the object will take exactly the same time to reach this level, when its speed will again be zero.

The formula $t = \sqrt{\dfrac{2h}{32}}$ (which is derived from our previous formula) connects the vertical distance of fall or rise with the time taken, where *t* is the time in seconds and *h* the height in feet. Therefore, when an object drops 144 ft, the time taken is:

$$\sqrt{\frac{2 \times 144}{32}} \text{ secs} = \sqrt{\frac{288}{32}} \text{ secs} = \sqrt{\frac{9}{1}} \text{ secs} = 3 \text{ secs.}$$

Similarly, if a high-jumper rises 4 ft from take-off to the high point of his jump (and this would be an exceptional effort) the time taken will be:

$$\sqrt{\frac{2 \times 4}{32}} \text{ secs} = \sqrt{\frac{8}{32}} \text{ secs} = \sqrt{\frac{1}{4}} \text{ secs} = \frac{1}{2} \text{ sec.}$$

The following are the periods of time for the performing of fancy

* In metric units, 9.8 metres

Motion

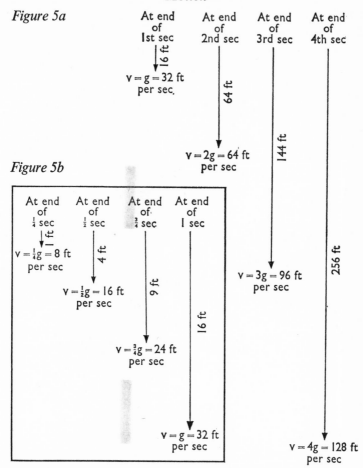

Figure 5a

At end of 1st sec — $v = g = 32$ ft per sec.

At end of 2nd sec — $v = 2g = 64$ ft per sec

At end of 3rd sec — $v = 3g = 96$ ft per sec

At end of 4th sec — $v = 4g = 128$ ft per sec

Figure 5b

At end of $\frac{1}{4}$ sec — $v = \frac{1}{4}g = 8$ ft per sec

At end of $\frac{1}{2}$ sec — $v = \frac{1}{2}g = 16$ ft per sec

At end of $\frac{3}{4}$ sec — $v = \frac{3}{4}g = 24$ ft per sec

At end of 1 sec — $v = g = 32$ ft per sec

Board (metres)	Height C. of G. raised from take-off	C. of G. time above board	C. of G. time below board	Time for whole flight	Speed of entry
1	4 ft	1·16 sec	Hands enter as C. of G. passes board	1·16 sec	15 m.p.h.
3	4 ft	1·16 sec	0·28 sec	1·44 sec	20 m.p.h.
3	1 ft	0·75 sec	0·33 sec	1·08 sec	18 m.p.h.
3	2 ft	0·91 sec	0·30 sec	1·21 sec	19 m.p.h.
5	2 ft	0·91 sec	0·50 sec	1·41 sec	23 m.p.h.
10	2 ft	0·91 sec	0·92 sec	1·83 sec	32 m.p.h.

dives from boards of competition height, based on the assumption that the diver's Centre of Gravity is the same height above the board at take-off as it is above the water at the moment of entry.* Speeds of entry are also given (on page 17).

Parallelogram and resolution of velocities

In the course of taking a running stride, high-jumping or releasing a shot (to take only three of countless examples) (Fig. 6) an athlete imparts to his body and/or the missile two motions simultaneously— one upward and the other forward. These are called *component velocities* because combined together, they produce a *resultant velocity*, i.e. the actual velocity of the body or missile. These two simultaneous component motions do not affect each other, can be considered separately, and for the purpose of athletic analysis it is often useful to treat them as such.

Figure 6   a   b   c

If the magnitude of each of these components is known, then both the direction and magnitude of the resultant velocity can be illustrated diagrammatically by the parallelogram method (Fig. 7). A spot is first marked on paper representing the point of release (in throwing) or the Centre of Gravity (see page 52) (in running, jumping and vaulting). From this two lines called *vectors* (from the Latin verb meaning to carry or convey) are drawn at right angles to each other; these indicate the two components, the length of each line from its point of origin to the arrowhead representing the magnitude of each velocity (Fig. 7a).

Using these as two sides of a parallelogram, the missing sides are

* A. F. Ball, 'The Mechanics of Diving'. Unpublished thesis; Loughborough College, England.

constructed by simple geometric methods (Fig. 7*b*). A diagonal is finally drawn from the point of origin to the opposite corner, representing in its length and direction both the magnitude and direction of the resultant velocity (Fig. 7*c*).

Figure 7   a   b   c

Conversely, when the magnitude and direction of the resultant motion are known it is simple enough to resolve this into its vertical and horizontal components (Fig. 8).

Component motions do not always operate at right angles to each other (see Fig. 168). In determining a resultant the parallelogram method can also be applied when angles are obtuse or acute (Fig. 9*a* and *b*). Here it is important to note that in the resolving of a resultant either the directions or the magnitudes of both components, or the direction and magnitude of one component, must be known in advance. Otherwise the problem is capable of many different solutions, since there are many parallelograms with the same diagonal.

Figure 8

a   b   *Figure 9*

Quantities like velocity which have both magnitude and direction (e.g. force, acceleration and momentum), are also called 'vector quantities' and can be combined by the parallelogram method. Other qualities (e.g. speed and kinetic energy) which have only *size*, without specific

19

direction, are called *scalars*. Track distances are usually treated as scalar quantities. We speak of a runner as having covered a distance regardless of the direction in which he travels. (See also pages 39–43.)

Path of Projectiles

As soon as throwing implements are released or athletes break contact with the ground they begin to fall, in the sense that gravity then changes their direction of motion. Hence, greater distance in throwing or jumping can be obtained when the initial velocity contains an upward as well as a forward component. For in this case the missile or athlete is in the air longer, permitting greater horizontal travel before return to ground.

Figure 10

Figure 11

In air-free space a combination of inclined-upward initial velocity and gravity causes the object's Centre of Gravity (see page 52) to describe a perfectly regular curve called a *parabola*. When the emphasis is on horizontal motion, as in long-jumping (Fig. 10), the curve is long and low, but in the high jump, where vertical movement is stressed, it is short and steep (Figs. 11 and 12).

Figure 12

It is important to note that in track and field athletics, where neither jet propulsion (where force is derived from the reaction to escaping gases) nor a mid-air change in weight take place, the movements of an athlete off the ground cannot disturb the smooth curve of his Centre of Gravity.

Again, in air-free space the horizontal component remains constant

21

throughout flight; the long-jumper's forward speed on landing will be the same as at take-off. However, the vertical component, being subject to the laws of freely falling bodies, will be zero at the high point of the jump or throw and then the athlete or missile will fall with gravitational acceleration.

In fact, a jumper or missile may be regarded as having two independent motions (Fig 12); an initial, uniform inclined-upward motion continuing along the line AB, and a free-fall measured at successive points (here, at $\frac{1}{8}$ second intervals) along this line. (The units 1, 4, 9, 16, etc., in Fig. 12 are units of 3 inches.)

Note that our high jumper moves *horizontally* at a steady speed, while a decreasing upward motion to the high point of his jump is matched by an increasing downward motion from then on.

Fig. 11 shows how, through the use of vectors (page 18), the proportion of a jumper's horizontal and vertical motion can be illustrated at any point along the flight path of his Centre of Gravity. Thus, at point A, the *tangent* AB (i.e. the straight line at right angles to the radius of the flight path at this point) represents the athlete's velocity *at that instant*; while the vectors AC and AD denote his horizontal and vertical velocities, respectively.

Note that while the horizontal components AC and WY are equal, the vertical velocities (at points A and W) differ not only in direction, but also in magnitude.

Figure 13

In practice, of course, an object in flight pushes air aside, encountering air resistance, a force which slows down motion and blunts the flight path, causing the Centre of Gravity to travel in a curve, somewhat as shown in Fig. 13. Air resistance depends upon the size, shape, spin and velocity of the moving object, but in jumping and throwing events it is sufficiently negligible for flight paths to be considered regular, i.e. parabolic.

The optimum angle for the projection of a missile, no matter what its velocity, is 45 deg., when its vertical and horizontal component velocities will be equal.* If projected at a greater or lesser angle the object falls short of its maximum range. But 45 deg. is the optimum

Figure 14

angle only when the points of release and landing are level (Fig. 14) which, in track and field athletics, is seldom so.

Fig. 15 illustrates diagrammatically how, in releasing the shot from a point 7 ft above the ground, the optimum angle varies with the

Figure 15

velocity; a low velocity necessitates the use of a comparatively low release angle, and vice versa. On the other hand, Fig. 16 shows how a short man, theoretically, must put more steeply than a tall one and use more velocity to attain a given distance. It is, therefore, upon *height* and *velocity* of release that optimum angles depend.

In the long-jump, where the athlete relies mainly on controlled sprinting speed to build up a high take-off velocity, this is done at the expense of vertical speed, horizontal motion being so marked that in the best jumps the athlete's Centre of Gravity (see page 52) is projected at take-off at an angle below 30 deg. (see page 165). Here, as in shot

* In long-distance projection (e.g. gunnery) other factors modify this, e.g. the curvature of the earth's surface, the manner in which its speed of rotation varies with latitude, air resistance (which varies with height and temperature), the strength and direction of the wind, the motion of any object aimed at and (e.g. in naval gunnery) the motion of the object carrying the means of projection.

Figure 16

putting, the point of projection of the Centre of Gravity is above the landing level.

The release angle in throwing the hammer is only fractionally below 45 deg., but aerodynamic considerations greatly affect release angles in the discus and javelin events, and are discussed in the chapter on Throwing (page 188).

CHAPTER THREE

Forces (1): Newton's Laws

Force is the effect one body has upon another. Motion in athletics can be produced only when force has been applied, but it is nevertheless possible to have force without motion. In track and field athletics the main sources of force are (*a*) internal, the muscular actions of the athlete, and (*b*) external, the downward pull of gravity, the friction and upthrust of the ground and the resistance of the air. As Sir Isaac Newton's Laws of Motion are fundamental to the whole science of force—even today's rocket and missile discoveries are based upon his theories—they will be discussed first.*

Newton's First Law (Law of Inertia)

It was as long ago as 1687 that Newton enunciated the first of his three laws in the now famous words:

'Every body continues in its state of rest, or of uniform motion in a straight line, except in so far as it may be compelled by impressed forces to change that state.'

This is known as the Law of Inertia, inertia (the Latin for idleness or laziness) being the property innate in all bodies, animate and inanimate, by virtue of which they obey this law.

Expressed in simpler language, it says that everything in the universe is lazy, so lazy that force is necessary to get it on the move, when it then travels in a straight line; so lazy that, once in motion, further force must be applied to slow it down, stop it, speed it up or change its direction.

Thus, a shot rolling along level ground would continue to roll for ever in a straight line were it not for ground and air friction. An athlete moving through space would continue to travel for ever in a

---

* The discrepancies that exist between Newtonian (i.e. classical) mechanics and the physical universe are quite undetectable by ordinary means and, generally speaking, are important only in investigating the motions of bodies of sub-atomic size or those with a speed approaching that of light. As Albert Einstein himself wrote, 'No-one must think that Newton's great creation can be overthrown by Relativity or any other theory.'

25

straight path were it not for air resistance and the downward pull of gravity. The law applies also to spinning motion. A hammer thrower would go on and on turning were it not for friction and the forces subsequently applied in releasing the missile.

Direct proof of the correctness of Newton's assumption is impossible here on earth, since we cannot remove a body completely from external influences, but in its logical results the law is never at variance with experience.

Inertia, therefore, is concerned with a body's resistance to change in movement and is an important—often determining—factor in problems involving energy-expenditure and fatigue in exercise. It is a property always present in an object and is never 'overcome' (*in the sense that it is destroyed*) once that object has been set in motion, as is frequently supposed.

The claim 'to get an object on the move one must overcome its inertia' is based on the common experience whereby it is more difficult to start an object moving than to keep it in motion; but this is due to the fact that, to start it, force must be used against both its inertia *and* the frictional ground and air forces, whereas to maintain a constant speed only the frictional forces oppose movement, and less force is therefore required. But to increase the speed again, inertia has still to be 'overcome'. For example, ignoring ground and air friction, when a definite force is applied horizontally, the pressure between the hand and a 16-lb shot is exactly the same, whether the shot is moved from rest or is in motion at the time. *In terms of inertia, therefore, rest and uniform straight-line motion are manifestations of the same thing.*

Inertia is proportional to *mass*—the amount of the material of which an object is made. In fact, the terms are often interchangeable. The mass of an object is the measure of its inertia, its resistance to change in motion. The British unit of mass is the pound (lb).* By way of illustration, if equal forces are applied to a 16-lb shot and a 1-lb 12¼-oz javelin, the change in motion of the javelin (i.e. its acceleration) will be much greater. Mass must not be confused with *weight*; we shall see later (page 50) that they are not the same.

Newton's Second Law (Law of Acceleration)

By means of the second law, which actually includes the first, we can

---

* In most American textbooks the unit quantity of mass is called the 'slug' which is that mass which will be accelerated at the rate of one foot per second per second by a force of one pound weight. A 'slug' is therefore approximately 32lb.

determine how force can change the motion of an object. It states:

'*The rate of change of momentum is proportional to the impressed force, and the actual change takes place in the direction in which the force acts.*'

Momentum is the product of mass and velocity: it can be considered as a measure of the quantity of motion possessed by a body. It is a vector quantity, i.e. it possesses both magnitude and direction. A runner having a mass of 140 lb and a velocity of 30 ft per second has a momentum of 4,200 units, and so has a 30-lb object moving at 140 ft per second. Thus, a marble can possess the momentum of a cannon ball, given sufficient velocity.

At a definite time the moving runner has momentum, and a period of time is necessary for him to change it. From the law of inertia we know that the velocity of a moving object (i.e. the distance it travels per unit of time in a given direction) remains constant unless a force acts on it. This second law tells us that, provided we consider a definite period of time, any change in velocity (positive or negative) will be directly proportional to the amount of force used; it will also be inversely proportional to the object's mass.

For example, consider a definite period of time, say, two seconds; the effective force a runner must use to increase his speed during these two seconds in a race is in direct proportion to his speed increase, i.e. if he wishes to double this speed increase in the two seconds he must double the amount of force he exerts.

If there are two runners, one weighing only half as much as the other, and the same effective horizontal force is exerted by each during the two seconds, the lighter athlete will acquire double the speed increase of the heavier one—demonstrating that the change in velocity is inversely proportional to the mass of the object. This second law therefore generalises the obvious fact that one can throw a cricket ball farther and faster than a 16-lb shot. (See also page 34.)

It should be noted, however, that a force need not act through an object's Centre of Gravity to produce a given linear acceleration, for the force will create the same linear acceleration whether or not so directed. Should the force *not* pass through the Centre of Gravity, that point will change speed in a direction parallel to the direction of the force while, simultaneously, the object will rotate about an axis passing through its Centre of Gravity (see also 'Moments in Rotation and Spin,' pages 69–71).

Newton's Third Law (Law of Reaction)*

For every force acting anywhere there is always an equal force acting in an opposite direction. Forces always work in pairs, as 'twins' opposing each other. This is the meaning of Newton's Third Law, which states:

'To every action there is an equal and opposite reaction; or the mutual actions of two bodies in contact are always equal and opposite in direction.'

The effect upon one body is known as the *action* and that upon the other the *reaction*, but it is often a matter of choice or opinion as to which is which. In mechanics the two forces are of equal importance and exist simultaneously; but obviously, in the analysis of human motion we have often to think of *Man* as originating the force.

To the question, 'Why don't the opposing forces cancel out, leaving no force at all?' the answer is that they *do* when they arise *in the same body*. That is why a body is unaffected by mutual actions between its parts. In athletics, however, this Third Law often involves equal and opposite forces *in two separate bodies*.

For example, if two spring balances are hooked together and then

Figure 17

Figure 18

Figure 19

* Newton's own, particular contribution to the theory of motion; for the First and Second Laws had been effectively applied earlier by Galileo.

pulled in opposite directions (Fig. 17) the readings on them will be identical. A man standing on the ground is pulled down on it with his weight and the ground pushes up with a force (often referred to as *ground reaction*) equal to his weight (Fig. 18). When a bird beats downward with its wings in flight, its body and the air struck experience equal but opposite forces (Fig 19). And when a sprinter leaves his blocks (Fig. 20) he drives backward with a force equal to that which propels him forward.

Figure 20   *Figure 21*

For as long as a runner or jumper *accelerates* his swinging leg upward at take-off, the tendency will be for the rest of his body to be pulled down; hence he could be considered effectively heavier at that instant (Fig. 21). If the leg ceases to accelerate, but continues upward with a uniform motion, then his take-off foot presses against the ground with a force equal to this weight; *and when it slows down momentarily he loses weight again.* In a reverse movement, with the leg dropping (but with his other foot still in contact with the ground) the pressure between his supporting foot and the ground decreases and then increases. These examples of action and reaction and the two-way action of forces can be demonstrated on a weighing machine or, more scientifically, on a force platform. (For a more detailed treatment of this, see Chapter 8, pages 149–54.)

When a force sets an object in motion the momentum of that object is altered. As, according to this Third Law, forces always work in opposing pairs, a change in momentum in one object must be accompanied by the same change in momentum of another object in an opposite direction and *the momentum of the system as a whole therefore remains the same.* Hence, when a gun is fired, the explosion gives the bullet momentum in a forward direction equal but opposite to the gun's 'kick' against the shoulder(Fig. 22).

Again, a high-jumper's momentum at take-off is equal to the change

$F2 = FI$

Figure 22

in the earth's momentum in an opposite direction (Fig. 11). But the reaction of the earth is not noticeable because of its enormous mass. Likewise, such is the law of reaction, the earth moves up to meet the athlete as he falls towards the earth. The earth's mass is so great in comparison that both movements can be neglected.

The principle holds good, too, for mid-air movements of parts of an athlete's body. Although, in the air, he can do nothing to change the momentum of his body as a whole (see *Path of projectiles*, page 20) nevertheless he can move a part of it against some other part, producing similar reactions within the body. These are discussed more fully in Chapter Five (pages 98–119).

It should be noted, however, that to exert a *maximum* of body force in running, jumping or throwing the athlete must be in contact with firm, resisting ground. If, for example, in shot putting he breaks contact before completing the delivery, then he can only impart additional speed to the shot by giving his body backward speed in reaction. In this case his final arm thrust is made at the cost of reducing the shoulder's forward speed; thus, the force and range of arm movement are reduced (pages 188–93 and 222).

Forces (2)

Force

As stated in the introduction to the previous chapter, force is the effect that one body has upon another.

In athletics all motion is derived from force—force from muscle tensions, from gravity, from the friction and upthrust of the ground and the resistance of the air. In sport we are concerned mostly with the use of force for *changing the state of motion* of athletes and their implements—slowing them down, stopping or speeding them up.

However, there can be force without motion. For example, a javelin or pole can be gripped tightly without its moving; a tennis ball can be flattened a little by squeezing. *Force can, therefore, bring about, or tend to bring about, a change of shape in a body*, causing stresses within, which are the result of its attempt to regain its original shape; *and forces do not affect motion when their resultant is zero.*

Force can be felt but not seen. But its effects can be seen and measured, and it can be described and determined in terms of its *magnitude, direction* and *point of application*. Like velocity and momentum, therefore, *it is a vector quantity*, and can be analysed by the use of a parallelogram.

Magnitude. Force is usually measured in pound-wt, a pound-wt being the pull of gravity on a standard pound of mass measured at the National Physical Laboratory, Teddington, Middlesex, England. Internally, the athlete obtains his force through the tension of muscle fibres. Each fibre, though sometimes several inches in length, is not more than a fraction of an inch in diameter. At rest, these fibres are soft, flabby and easily stretched, but on receiving nerve impulses they shorten, or attempt to shorten, changing in effect from a piece of perished rubber to a contracted steel spring.

The magnitude of muscle force is in direct proportion to (a) the size and number of fibres exerting tension, (b) the speed at which active fibres are *forced* to lengthen, in what is known as an *eccentric contraction* (i.e. when the muscle is loaded sufficiently to lengthen *even though it is trying to shorten*): and force is inversely proportional to (c) the speed with which fibres are *allowed* to shorten (i.e. in *concentric contraction*).

Paradoxically, maximum tension seems to be developed when active muscle is stretched quickly. In athletics this 'priming' of muscle is usually brought about by (a) quickly lowering the body on ground contact, (b) abruptly checking its horizontal motion, or (c) otherwise increasing its load by accelerating another part of the body (e.g. a leg, the arms, the hips, or the trunk).

Thus, a high jumper is able to exert greater force at take-off through a bracing and rapid involuntary flexing of his jumping leg before straightening that leg in powerful recoil (Fig. 140*k-o*). A golfer's trunk is already twisting in the direction of his drive before his club-head reaches its highest point in the back-swing (Fig. 23). Likewise, good throwers 'lead with the hips' to first stretch resisting trunk muscles (Fig. 190 *d-e*).

That rare phenomenon, an *isometric contraction* (where muscle tension is exactly balanced by opposing forces in a static situation) does *not* produce the greatest tensions, as has been supposed.*

In muscles with straight parallel fibres (e.g. the sartorious) force potential can be estimated by measuring the proportional fibre cross section (*proportional*, not actual, because muscle also contains blood vessels, connective tissues, inter-spaces, etc.) in terms of pounds per square inch.

Figure 23

However, in muscles with a 'belly' (e.g. the gastrocnemius) maximum force, for a given length and weight, can be much greater—but at the expense of less shortening; because the fibres run obliquely and, therefore, for only a fraction of the muscle's full anatomical length. In this case the cross section is usually impossible to define.

Through training, an athlete cannot increase the number of fibres within a

Figure 24

---

* D. W. Grieve, 'Stretching active muscle and leading with the hips' (*Coaching Review*, 7, 1, June 1969, Royal Canadian Legion); E. W. Banister, 'Theories of Strength Training' (*Coaching Review*, 4, 2, September 1966, Royal Canadian Legion).

Forces (2)

muscle but he can increase its force potential by increasing their diameter. Here, the two-way effect of force is again in evidence, since a muscle pulls as powerfully upon its origin as on its insertion, but in an opposite direction (Fig. 24).

In athletics we are seldom, if ever, concerned with the measurement of force of a single muscle, but rather think in terms of a whole movement, momentarily involving the total force of several muscle groups working against the resistance of the ground (as in running), a missile (e.g. in discus throwing) or, sometimes, against some other part of the body (as in movement which originates in the air).

Certainly, in athletic movement, no muscle—and not even a single muscle group—works alone, for all the muscles of the body are more or less in constant demand, supporting, guiding and generally contributing to force and the control of movement. Where, through weakness in the supporting muscles, joints are poorly stabilized, proper running, jumping and throwing movement is impossible; and in such activities as weight training (where great resistance to the body's natural rotational patterns is developed) such weakness can cause the body to be moved out of effective position.

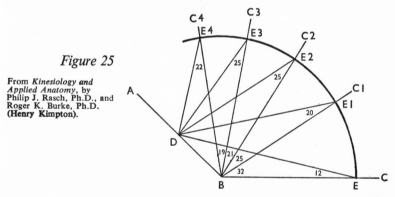

Figure 25

From *Kinesiology and Applied Anatomy*, by Philip J. Rasch, Ph.D., and Roger K. Burke, Ph.D. (Henry Kimpton).

Fig. 25 illustrates the changes in the angle of pull when a muscle shortens. The line AB represents a stationary bone and BC a moving one. With the bone-lever at BC the angle of pull DEB is only 12 deg., but when the bone is moved to BC1 the angle increases to 20 deg.; it is 25 deg. at both BC2 and BC3 and then reduces to 22 deg. at position BC4. Only when the muscle's origin D is farther from the axis B than the insertion E can this angle be at right angles.

Direction. When athletic efficiency is at its best force has been properly directed both internally and externally. The direction of the force exerted by a single muscle (Fig. 25) depends upon the relation of

33

the moving bone's long axis to the muscle-insertion. The angle between the muscle's line of pull and the long axis of this bone (the axis being a straight line from the bone's mid-point at either end) is known as the angle of pull, an angle which, with body movement, is constantly changing.

From a purely mechanical point of view, a muscle's most effective pull will be at right angles to the moving bone; but as muscle fibres at such an angle are seldom fully stretched, the greatest effective force is usually obtained when the angle of pull is more acute (Fig. 25). It would seem, therefore, that *physiological laws sometimes work in opposition to mechanical ones,* which points to the futility of trying to analyse athletic techniques on a mechanical basis, muscle by muscle.

As with the assessing of the magnitude of force, it is therefore more convenient to consider the direction of an athlete's *total, resultant* body force exerted against the resistance of the ground or apparatus. In running, for example, this should be done in such a way as to produce mainly horizontal movement; at take-off in high-jumping force must be directed mainly in a downward direction, so that the athlete shall be thrown almost vertically; and in throwing events the direction of total body force will determine the angle at which the missiles are thrown.

Point of application. The effect of force varies with the point of its application. This characteristic is discussed more fully later (pages 64–6 and 69–77). Meanwhile, it is sufficient to say that, internally, force is applied to the bone levers at the points where muscles originate or are inserted (Fig. 24). As to the total force of propulsion in running and jumping, it is applied where the feet contact the ground (Fig. 20) and, in shot putting, where the missile touches the hand (Fig. 189). The point of application and the direction of force may be combined in the one concept: *the line of action.*

Accelerated motion

As already stated, in track and field athletics we are mostly concerned with the use of force to change the state of motion of athletes and their implements. In this connection, two simple experiments should help to clarify its effects.

First, as in Fig. 26a, two 8-lb shots are placed on a smooth, horizontal surface, and between them is set a compressed spring which cannot expand because it is tied. When the thread is broken the spring drives both shots apart with equal force (Fig. 26b) and they collide simul-

34

Figure 26

taneously with two wooden blocks set, beforehand, at equal distances from the shots' original positions (Fig. 26c). From this it can be seen that *when equal forces are applied against equal masses they produce the same change in velocity*, and experiments prove that *accelerations given to a body are proportional to the magnitude of the force.*

Then, one of the shots is replaced by a 16-lb missile (Fig. 27a) and the experiment is repeated (Fig.27b). Now, the larger shot is given only half the acceleration of the smaller one and, in a given time, it travels only half the distance (Fig. 27c). From this we can conclude that *when equal forces impart accelerations to unequal masses, the product of mass and acceleration is the same*; which gives us our measurement of *force = mass × acceleration.*

Therefore, under otherwise identical conditions, the acceleration of athletes and their apparatus depends upon their masses which, in turn, are measures of *inertia*, resistance to motion (Newton's First and Second Laws, pages 25–7).

To provide *equal acceleration* in *unequal masses*, the forces applied must be proportional to the masses; for example, if there are two runners, one weighing 250 lb and the other 125 lb, the heavier athlete must exert twice the force of the lighter athlete to produce the same acceleration.

Frictional forces apart, *any* force will accelerate *any* mass. For

Figure 27

example, but for the resistance of air and water a docker leaning against the side of an Atlantic liner, unmoored, could give it motion with which to cross to America—but he would have to lean in the right direction and the crossing would take a long time! In practice, of course, liners can be moved only when the force acting on them in a given direction is greater than the frictional and other forces opposing; and so it is with athletes and their apparatus.

Just as the Force of Gravity is responsible for a constant free-fall acceleration which, in 1, 2, 3, etc. units of time produces vertical distances in the proportions of 1, 4, 9, etc. (pages 15–17) so does a similar relationship between time and distance apply to an object or athlete moving *in any direction* as a result of the application of *any constant force in* that direction.

Impulse

The change in speed of an athlete, discus, shot, javelin or hammer does not merely depend upon the force applied, but also upon the *time* for which it operates, its *impulse.* In starting from blocks, for example, an athlete should adjust his position not only to increase his driving force but also to lengthen the time during which it is exerted, thus increasing his starting velocity (Fig. 130). And in the throwing events, also, the best techniques are those in which maximum muscular force is exerted for the longest possible time.

The same change in speed (and, therefore, the same impulse) can be produced by a small force acting for a long time, or a very large force acting for a short time. However, in athletics, an increase in force often requires a more rapid action, resulting in a decrease in *time* of operation—unless the distance over which the force operates is increased.

The impulse of a force is equal to the momentum (mass × velocity) of the mass moved from rest by the force. Of academic interest only, the impulse given to a high-jumper at take-off is also given to the earth, but in an opposite direction. Their momenta are therefore equal. Likewise, an athlete's momentum from the blocks in a sprint start is equal but opposite to the earth's, for the impulse is the same. In fact, *the concept of momentum is often used as equivalent to that of impulse.*

In the analysis of athletic movement it is often convenient to distinguish between a *controlled* impulse, due to direct muscular effort and joint leverage, as with the leg-drive in sprint-starting, and a *transmitted* impulse produced, for example, by the bracing of a comparatively unyielding leg against the ground during the initial stages of a high-jump take-off, where its magnitude and direction cannot be determined through muscular action of the leg itself (Fig. 99). Almost invariably, *in track and field athletic techniques transmitted impulses precede the smaller controlled impulses.* (See also pages 149–54). Because it involves force, impulse is a vector quantity.

Effective force

In track and field athletics there are many examples of the impossbility of exerting full force against a fast-moving object, for the feet (in running) and the hand (in throwing) cannot be moved fast enough. In such cases, the speed of movement of the source of resistance reduces not only the ability to apply muscular effort, but also the time for which that effort can be applied. These two factors may place quite a low limit to the size of the *effective force*, i.e. the force 'received' by the ground or implement. For this reason, in most athletic events, acceleration has its greatest value at the beginning, when the athlete's body and/or the missile he holds is moving slowly.

Sprinting is a good example. At the start, where the opposing force of air resistance is small because the athlete's movement over the ground is comparatively slow, most of the considerable horizontal force of his leg drive is effective in producing a marked change in speed. But as his speed increases the opposing forces also increase, and therefore a progressively smaller fraction of his limited leg drive is available to add to his speed.

It is difficult to exert a forceful backward thrust against the ground which, to the athlete, appears to be moving in an opposite direction. Top speed is reached when the effective force of the leg drive equals all the opposing forces. Up to this point in the race his speed has increased, but by a progressively diminishing degree. For, with each stride taken, foot contact is of shorter and shorter duration; impulse is successively reduced and even without an actual reduction in horizontal thrust (and reduction is certain) each successive increase in speed is smaller.

A second example can be taken from shot putting where, as soon as the movement across the circle begins, pressure between the shot and the athlete's fingers increases; for force is being applied to accelerate it, and this pressure will always be equal to the force exerted. A further increase in applied force would result in another increase in pressure, but in practice shot putters find the pressure *reduced* in the final arm-thrust; they find it *easier* to move, whereas if it were possible to impart a constant acceleration it would be as difficult to put at the end as at

37

the beginning. This is because of the difficulty of 'keeping up with' the shot.

In fact, to be able to accelerate his body or a throwing implement an athlete must be capable of moving at a greater speed than the ground or the missile moving away from him. And the greater his speed, in comparison, the greater his effective force will be. Clearly, then, *the ability of an athlete to apply force depends not only upon strength but also upon speed.* (See also pages 69–71, 'Moments in Rotation and Spin.')

Summation of forces

From a purely mechanical point of view it is immaterial whether a succession of forces is applied one by one or simultaneously; the resultant is the same. However, where human beings are concerned the strongest parts of the body are the heaviest, and have a correspondingly greater inertia: consequently they are less speedy in their movements. With the athlete it is a question of using the different muscles when they are capable of sufficient speed to apply full force.

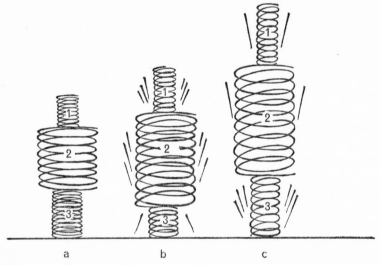

a   b   c

Figure 28

The numbered springs represent a high jumper's arms (1), trunk and free leg (2), and jumping leg (3). In (A) the spring-system is at rest. In (B) very considerable upward accelerations of the free leg, trunk and arms place a heavy burden on the supporting leg—tending to compress it. Only when these accelerations are reduced (*reduced*, not finished, if the greatest possible impulse is to be exerted against the ground) can the jumping leg extend (C).

Forces (2)

Again, because the force exerted externally by muscle is inversely proportional to the speed of its contraction, both *force* and *time*—the constituents of *impulse*—can be increased *through the simultaneous action of various muscles and levers. For, then, each is prevented from moving more rapidly by the accelerations of others.*

These two factors call for a definite sequence and timing of body forces. Although, for maximum impulse, all parts of an athlete's body should, in theory, commence their accelerations simultaneously, *in practice* the strongest but slower muscles surrounding the body's Centre of Gravity begin, to be joined by the trunk and thighs and then by the weaker, lighter but faster extremities—*ideally, with all the forces ending together.* This principle, as it applies to high jumping, is illustrated in Fig. 28.

Of course, the sequence with which an athlete uses the different parts of his body is partly dependent upon the nature of the construction of the human body; and the timing of the various movements can be influenced by the strengths and accelerations of these parts (*see* also pages 189 and 221).

Opposing forces, parallelogram and resolution of forces

As already stated (page 31) the qualities determining a force are its magnitude, direction and point of application. Force is a vector quantity, therefore, which can be represented diagrammatically by straight lines, as can motion (page 18). Indeed, as, in athletics, all motion is derived through the application of force, many claims made in Chapter Two in respect of motion apply equally well here.

A line can be drawn, called a *force vector*, with one end representing the point of application, its direction and arrowhead coinciding with the direction of the force, and its length containing as many units of length as the force has units of force (Fig. 7).

Opposing forces. In Fig. 29 (tug o' war) the reactions to the forces exerted on the ground are represented by vector lines, both horizontal, which can be replaced by a single line—a resultant—representing the 50 lb acting towards the right. When two forces are acting in opposite directions, therefore, the resultant has the direction of the larger force.

Parallelogram of forces. But when several forces acting at a point are not directly opposed and parallel, the problem is more difficult. Forces, like velocities, do not disturb each other; each is separate, and for purposes of analysing movement in athletics it is often convenient to treat them as such.

200 lbs

250 lbs

50 lbs

Figure 29

To take, for example, the directing of a runner's propulsive, muscular force against gravity and air resistance, the relevant point of action of these three forces is the athlete's Centre of Gravity (Fig.30)—a point where, it can be assumed, all the mass of his body is concentrated. (This is discussed more fully on page 52.) At a constant speed these three forces balance each other.

Both gravity (CA) working vertically downwards, and air resistance (CB) acting horizontally against the runner are represented by force vectors. Using these as two sides of a parallelogram, the missing sides are constructed geometrically and a diagonal is drawn from the point of origin—i.e. the Centre of Gravity—to the opposite corner (CD). This line represents in both length and direction the magnitude and direction of the combined opposing forces. The propulsive muscular force required to maintain a constant speed is therefore represented by the line CE. This, an *equilibrant* needed to balance the other forces, is not

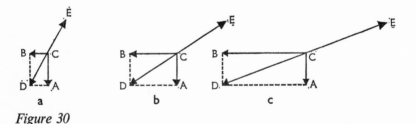

Figure 30

Fig. 30*a, b, c*, above, illustrates the directing of a runner's propulsive force against the force of gravity and air resistance. Point C represents the athlete's Centre of Gravity, the line CA the force of gravity, the lines CB three strengths of air resistance and the lines CD the magnitude and direction of the resultant of the opposing forces. The propulsive force required to maintain a constant speed is represented by the line CE.

Forces (2)

necessarily to be identified with the angle of the trunk—the runner's 'body-lean'—but none the less Fig.30b and c show the need for greater emphasis on horizontal force when air resistance is increased.

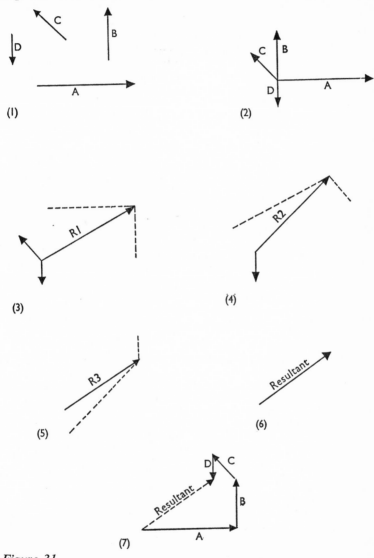

Figure 31
(After Figs.2–25 and 2–26 of *Physics for the Enquiring Mind*, E. M. Rogers, Princeton University Press, U.S.A.)

Where more than two forces act upon a point (as, for example, within an athlete's body during motion, when diverse muscular forces are involved) the resultant of two forces is first obtained in the manner already described and then this is combined vector by vector, until a resultant—a single force that can replace them all—is found.

In Fig. 31, for example, the vectors A, B, C and D (1) and (2) can be compounded by first adding C to R1 (3) (the resultant of A and B) to obtain R2 (4); and then by adding vector D (4), giving R3 (5) and (6). Or, more simply, these vectors can be added (in any order) head-to-tail —when their resultant will be the single vector joining start to finish. (Fig. 31). (7).

If the resultant is zero, the end of the tail-to-head pattern will be back at the starting point. (See also pages 18–20.)

Resolution of forces. In Fig 32*a* a long-jumper is shown at take-off with the line of action of a force driving him into the air from his jumping foot (the point of application). Two effects of this force are to project him vertically and accelerate him forward. We know that these component forces may be regarded separately, but in what proportions are they represented? The problem is the reverse of that discussed already.

Again, the geometrical parallelogram method is used; but either the directions or magnitudes of both components, or the direction and magnitude of one component, must be known in advance, otherwise (as there are many parallelograms with the same diagonal) the problem is capable of many different solutions. In this case we know the directions of the components. Two lines are then produced from the point of application (i.e. the foot), one vertical and the other horizontal, and a parallelogram is then made whose diagonal is the vector of the take-off force (Fig. 32*b*). The length of each of these lines in comparison with

a   b

Figure 32

that of the diagonal represents the magnitude of the components in relation to the take-off drive.

If the take-off force is known, of course, then the line of action can be drawn in units of length corresponding to the units of force, and from the length of the component vectors the magnitude of the horizontal and vertical forces can be calculated.

Work and energy

Work. The word 'work', as used in everyday life or in athletics, refers to the overcoming of resistance. No matter how hard and exhausting the struggle or the physical benefit derived therefrom, if an athlete attempts to lift a 300-lb barbell and fails—then he has done no mechanical work! For in order to do work, in the scientific sense, a force must move an object through some distance. *Work = Force × Distance.*

This formula can also be applied (somewhat academically, perhaps, from the point of view of the coach or athlete) to the working of a single muscle. If its force of contraction is unknown then this is computed from its proportional cross-section (see page 32) and the distance is represented by the distance through which the fibres shorten—a distance usually estimated at half their resting length.

Without equipment found only in the laboratory it is impossible to measure accurately the work done by athletes; for in such calculations great care must be taken to ensure that only the force acting in the direction of motion is considered, and to remember that the effective forces exerted in athletic movement are continually changing from one instant to another.

However, it is sometimes useful and of interest to make a rough assessment, measuring force in pound-wt and the distance in feet—calling the unit of work the foot-pound. Thus, from films it could be calculated approximately that a high-jumper applied his take-off force over a vertical distance of $1\frac{1}{2}$ ft before leaving the ground and if, say, it was estimated that he exerted a 350-lb force then his work at take-off would be $1\frac{1}{2} \times 350 = 525$ foot-pounds. Similarly, a javelin thrower who in the actual throwing action pulled the implement over a distance of 6 ft, using a 130-lb force, would do 780 foot-pounds of work, and so would another thrower applying 260 lb-wt over 3 ft.

Energy. Work must be performed in order to accelerate an athlete or throwing implement. Conversely, a moving athlete, discus, shot, hammer or javelin possesses a certain *capacity to do work* (called

43

energy) by giving up velocity, i.e. by coming to rest. The energy an object has by virtue of its motion is called *kinetic energy*; it is the kinetic energy of a javelin which drives it several inches into the ground; a hurdler's kinetic energy sends the hurdle flying when he hits it. This type of energy depends directly on the object's mass; for a given velocity, the greater mass will have more energy. It depends, too, on the square of the velocity; i.e. if an object's velocity is doubled then the kinetic energy becomes four times as great. In linear motion the kinetic energy of a body is given by the formula $e = \frac{1}{2}mv^2$, where v is the linear velocity of the mass. Unlike momentum, energy is a non-vectorial quantity, which explains why kinetic energy can be satisfactorily used, whatever its direction.

Figure 33

There is also the energy of position or condition—*potential energy*. A drawn bow (Fig.33) is ready to do work and therefore possesses potential energy. Likewise, a high-jumper in mid-air, a pole vaulter high up over the bar or a shot at the high point of its trajectory—all have potential energy by virtue of their positions.

It appears to be one of the natural laws that energy can be neither created nor destroyed. No machine—and no athlete—can use more energy than has already been absorbed.

Since energy is the capacity for doing work, it is measured in units of work—i.e. in foot-pounds. If, for example, an athlete during weight training lifts 200 lb 5ft off the floor, the barbell's potential energy is 200 × 5 or 1000 foot-pounds. If the barbell is then dropped, its potential energy is changed into the kinetic energy of motion, and at the instant of striking the ground it still has 1000 foot-pounds of kinetic energy; the potential energy has gone. But after the weight has struck the ground the kinetic energy disappears, to be changed into other forms of energy.

When track and field athletic techniques are performed on a sound mechanical basis they require the least possible expenditure of energy or, as in sprinting, enable athletes to utilise large amounts in short periods. However, in coaching the techniques of running, jumping, vaulting and throwing are best studied and analysed through the concept of *momentum* rather than energy.

Forces (2)

Power

In track and field athletics it is not merely the work performed which is important but also the time taken to do it; and in many events an athlete has very little time; a long-jumper moving at great horizontal speed over the eight-inch take-off board, for example, has but a fraction of a second in which to drive downward; he must work very quickly.

Even with regard to the development of strength and muscular endurance in training, *the rate of exercising* is important to athletes, for, as Steinhaus maintains in formulating the principle of progressive overloading, 'Muscle hypertrophy is in proportion, not to actual work done, but to the work done per unit of time.'*

In mechanics, the rate at which work is done is called *power*. Therefor *power = work ÷ time*. The *more work* that is done in a given time the greater the power; and the *quicker* it is done then the greater is the power used. Here it is important to note the difference between the more precise mechanical meaning and the word's looser meaning in everyday parlance—when, usually, it refers to force.

The measurement of power can be expressed in different ways, but kinesiologists, physiologists and others concerned with the analysis of human motion use the foot-pound per second as the smaller unit of measurement and the horse-power as the larger. It was James Watt, the Scottish inventor, who originally assessed the value of horse-power at 33,000 foot-pounds per minute, or 550 foot-pounds per second.†

To take a simple case: the horse-power of a man running up a flight of stairs can be calculated if his weight, time and the height of the stairs are known. If, then, he weighs 154 lb and takes 4 seconds to climb 14 ft, his rate of working (i.e. his horse-power) is:

$$\frac{154 \times 14}{550 \times 4} = 0 \cdot 98.$$

From a mechanical standpoint the measurement of power in track and field athletics is exceedingly difficult because, as already maintained, it is usually impossible to assess with accuracy the amount of work—in particular the ever-changing effective force of an athlete's

* A. H. Steinhaus, 'The Physiology of Exercise'. Series of lectures, Chicago. U.S.A., 1948.
† He tested horses to see how much weight they could lift, through what distance and in what time, pumping water out of coal-mines.

movement. In sprinting, for example, the distance run and time taken are easily come by, but how, without the most complicated of equipment, is the runner's effective force—which changes with each stride—to be calculated?

Even if it were possible to obtain such figures, the result would make no allowance for additional work against gravity, air resistance, ground friction, positive and negative acceleration of the limbs, and the internal resistances due to muscle viscosity and the friction of various body tissues one against another.

It is for this reason that physiologists find it more convenient to think in terms of the energy used in exercise, and have calculated from the rate of oxygen usage that an average sprinter at top speed develops approximately thirteen horse-power (see also page 133).

The ability to work quickly—i.e. powerfully—depends partly upon an athlete's neuro-muscular co-ordination and also upon his attitude of mind, e.g., the absence of inhibition through fear of failure or injury, his determination and concentration. However, although muscular effort has so often to be exerted as quickly as possible, it is essential not to lose sight of the importance of *range* in working. Misunderstanding often leads to an omission of whole phases of forceful movement in the build-up of speed. Thus, the athlete fails to attain maximum effect.

Centripetal and Centrifugal Forces

From Newton's Law of Inertia (page 25) we know that objects will continue to move in a straight path unless compelled by force to do otherwise. It follows, therefore, that when an athlete spins with a hammer (to take the best of countless examples in athletics) he must apply force to keep it moving in a near circular path.

By exerting this force—by pulling *on the hammer*—he accelerates it, even if it continues to move with only uniform speed, for by changing the hammer's *direction* of motion he is continually changing its velocity. But as soon as he lets go, the hammer continues steadily along at a tangent; its inertia makes it move in a straight line again, at right angles to the radius of motion at the point of release (Fig. 34).

The pulling-in force exerted by the athlete on the hammer is called *centripetal*, the equal but opposite reaction to which is a *centrifugal* force, acting on *the athlete*, pulling outward directly along the radius of motion (Fig. 35). Speaking generally, in athletics this centrifugal force is a by-product of an effort to increase rotational speed; in itself

Figure 34

Figure 35

it is seldom advantageous and is more often an embarrassment to an athlete.

The force required to keep an object moving in a circular path (and the equal but opposite centrifugal force) depends upon the *mass* and *speed* of the object and its *radius* of motion. Other things being equal, this force

(i) *is proportional to the moving mass.* Thus, a 16-lb hammer is pulled in (and, therefore, outward simultaneously) with twice the force of an 8-lb one;

(ii) *is proportional to the square of the velocity.* If the hammer's speed (i.e. the actual, linear speed) is doubled, the centripetal and centrifugal forces increase four-fold. That is, they are proportional *to the square of the angular velocity* (i.e. the angle described by the

hammer per second). For example, if angular velocity is increased three-fold then the hammer needs nine times the original force to be kept moving in a circular path, to which the reaction is nine times the original centrifugal force;

(iii) for a constant angular velocity, *is proportional to the radius of motion.* Again, with hammer throwing as our example: when two men turn with

Figure 36

the same angular velocity, the shorter man, with half the radius of motion of the taller, needs only half the centripetal force (and, therefore, half the centrifugal force) to control it.

In 'taking' a bend, a runner uses the track surface to supply the necessary centripetal force— which then thrusts sideways against his feet, threatening to topple him outwards. To avoid this he leans inwards.

On a banked curve (Fig. 37) there is less (perhaps no) need of this sideways friction; for a surface tilted sufficiently can then push the athlete straight out with a force AB, the vertical component of which, AC, counteracts his weight, while the horizontal component, AD, provides the necessary centripetal force.

Figure 37

If, momentarily, both man and hammer head are spinning with equal angular velocity about the axis shown (Fig. 36), their respective distances from the axis are inversely proportional to their masses; i.e. if the athlete weighs sixteen times as much as the hammer-head, his radius, relatively, will be sixteen times less (the measurements being made along each radius from the axis to each Centre of Gravity). Under such circumstances the centripetal force pulling on the hammer is equal to the centrifugal force pulling simultaneously on the athlete, but in an opposite direction. An increase in turning speed will increase both forces and there will be no cause to adjust the thrower's position (Fig. 35).

Since almost all athletic movement is angular in character, these principles apply to greater or lesser degree in all events. However, they have a particular significance in hammer and discus throwing and in the pole vault.

They apply too, to bend running, where athletes find it more difficult to sprint at top speed in an inside lane than in an outside one (Fig. 37).

Force of gravity

All athletic performance is influenced in some way by the force of gravity, a centripetal force 'by which bodies tend to the centre of the earth' (Newton.)* In Chapter Two (page 16) the acceleration of all

---

* He gave no first cause for Gravitation; modern science asks "what" and "how" without knowing the primary "why" for the behaviour of the Universe.

Forces (2)

freely falling bodies due to gravity was given as 32 ft per second each second—a figure sufficiently accurate for most calculations involved in an analysis of track and field techniques.

This might seem to violate Newton's First Law; for why should all objects accelerate vertically downwards at the same rate regardless of their masses if, when projected horizontally by an equal force, their accelerations are strictly determined by their masses? (See page 34.) The answer lies in the perfect balance of gravitation and inertia; *the earth always attracts an object with a force proportional to the mass of that object.* So, doubling the mass of the athlete would double the size of the force between him and the earth.*

However, although it is true that at a given point on the earth all bodies fall with the same acceleration, *the pull of gravity diminishes as the distance increases away from the earth's centre and is inversely proportional to the square of the distance.*† There is, therefore, a slight variation in gravitational acceleration between the poles and the equator (where the distance from the earth's centre, at sea level, is approximately 13 miles greater than at either pole) amounting to 0·54 per cent—just large enough to be detected. (Actually 0·3 per cent of the difference arises because the earth is spinning and, in consequence, a body at the equator tends to move off into space; there is a centrifugal effect.)

To date, most world athletic records have been made in the temperate zones, where the acceleration is 0·36 per cent greater than at the equator. Thus, a 26-ft long jump in Germany would be approximately 1¼ in. farther in, say, Kenya, and a 255-ft javelin throw in New Zealand is worth another 6½-in. in Ecuador.‡

The varying gravitational attractions of the sun and moon, which influence the tides, also affect the flight of objects—if only to an infinitesimal extent.

---

*The attractive force between an athlete and the earth depends not only on the mass of the athlete but on the mass of the earth as well, and is proportional to the *product* of their masses, i.e. these multiplied together.

†This '*inverse square law of gravitation*', almost certainly conceived by Newton in his mother's garden at Woolsthorpe, Lincolnshire, in 1666, '. . . was occasioned by the fall of an apple, as he sat in contemplative mood' (Stukeley, *Memoirs of Newton's Life*, pages 19–20). What Newton (then 23) saw was not that the apple must be drawn to the earth by Gravity. (That limited concept is at least as old as Aristotle). What *he* realised was that *all masses attract all other masses*; the same force reached out endlessly into space; the earth's attraction was not unique.

‡ G. T. P. Tarrant, 'Mechanics of Human and Animal Activity' (*School Science Review*, England, n. 78, December 1938, page 259).

Weight and density

In discussing Newton's Law of Inertia a distinction was made between *mass* and *weight* (page 26). The mass of an object is a measure of its inertia, its resistance to change in motion. This is a property which does not change from place to place; an athlete with 180 lb of mass would require as much force to obtain a given acceleration in Timbuctoo or Tooting, on the moon as here on earth.

However, because of the slight variation in pull, at the equator an athlete weighs 0·5 per cent less there than in the neighbourhood of the poles, and in the same way, weight, with the pull of gravity, decreases gradually with increasing height above sea-level.

On the moon our athlete would weight only 30 lb, for the gravitational pull there is about a sixth of the earth's. (Although the mass of the moon is only approximately an eightieth of the earth's, its diameter is considerably less and its surface, in consequence, is nearer its centre* Because of the inverse square law, the moon's gravity, per unit mass, is therefore relatively greater.) When we speak of 'weight', therefore, we refer to the force of attraction between an object and the earth—an attraction proportional to the object's mass. If we hold a 16-lb shot in our hand we must exert a certain muscular force to counteract the earth's attraction; this we call the shot's weight, but it *can* vary, if only fractionally.

Not all 16-lb shots are of the same size. Brass shots (which have a lead core) are smaller for their weight than iron ones; a 16-lb shot made from tungsten would be about the size of a tennis ball. Similarly, athletes of different sizes sometimes weigh the same, and vice versa. Obviously, therefore, objects vary in the ratio of their weight (and mass) to volume; i.e. they differ in their *density*. It is as though, in a denser body, matter is more closely packed. And, with the human body, the density of different parts will vary, e.g. bone is denser than blood.

Weightlessness

When a man stands erect on the ground, the force of gravity acting on his body (i.e. his weight) is cancelled out by an equal upward force exerted by the ground, i.e. '*ground reaction*'; otherwise, obviously, he would accelerate towards the earth's centre (see page 28). This condition also applies to the various *parts* of his body which, in the position

*It is approximately 3-11ths the distance from the surface of the earth to *its* centre.

Figure 38

shown (Fig. 38) have each to support the body weight above them. Thus, each part experiences a degree of compression which increases from the head downwards. This compression can be altered by a change in posture; e.g. increasing if the man stands on one leg (thereby doubling the vertically upward thrust through that leg) or if he accelerates some part of his body vertically.

However, when he breaks contact with the ground, gaining downward speed or losing upward speed at a rate of 32 ft per second every second, these states of compression, the sensations associated with them and their effect on the neuromuscular interactions controlling posture and directing movement no longer exist. (For example, in long-jumping, a clumsy initial attempt at a hitch-kick (Fig. 147) can be caused by 'not knowing where the legs are'—because of a lack of pressure on the receptors of the feet and a resulting poor kinesthetic feed-back.) His body, lacking ground reaction, then assumes a condition of transient *'weightlessness'* and can move its various parts, or objects carried by it, in ways which, in a vertical plane, would otherwise require greater effort —resistance to motion originated in the air being due only to inertia. In a state of 'free fall', for example, the man in the position shown (Fig. 38) will have no sensation of weight in his arms; from the standpoint of mechanics, it requires no effort to hold them in this position, since they and the rest of his body are experiencing the same gravitational accelera- tion. *Thus, the condition of 'weightlessness' tends to increase mobility at the expense of control, applying not only in jumping, diving and*

51

trampolining but even during those brief moments for which runners break contact with the ground on each stride.

It is interesting to note that when, after breaking ground contact, a man relaxes completely, he tends naturally to assume a position in which a state of angular equilibrium is reached between the different parts of his body, depending upon the mass and tonus of his various muscles. Fig. 39 illustrates the resulting posture*.

Note also that a floating swimmer (who must displace a weight of water equal to that of his whole body) does not experience 'weightlessness', because his limbs are supported externally—*water reaction* being substituted for *ground reaction.*

Experience of prolonged weightlessness in space has indicated the importance of gravity to human health. With the body no longer subject to its influence red blood corpuscles diminish, the blood collects in the thorax, muscles lose their tone while bones lose calcium and become more brittle.

Figure 39

Centre of gravity

We know that the earth attracts every tiny particle of an object with a gravitational force which is proportional to the mass of each particle. If all these separate attractions are thought of as being added together to make one resultant force—i.e. the weight of the object—the point where this force acts will be the *Centre of Gravity.*

In analysing track and field techniques such a point is often used to represent mass as a whole: the body mass of the athlete, a piece of apparatus, or the combined mass of athlete and implement, as in the pole vault or a throwing event. It is here that we can consider all the mass of the object to be concentrated; in fact, a centre of mass or weight from which the body could be suspended in perfect balance in any position.

However, it is important to realise that this point need not necessarily divide or be surrounded by equal masses. (Only when a body is of uniform density will its centre of gravity coincide with its centre of volume.) It is the product of each mass and its distance—i.e. the moments, or turning effects (see page 64)—which must be equal on either side of, or surrounding, the Centre of Gravity.

* John C. Simons, 'An introduction to surface-free behaviour' (*Ergonomics,* England, Vol. 7, No. 1. January 1964).

Forces (2)

Fig. 40 and the accompanying tables show the various Centres of Gravity and hinge-points for the male human body. (Note that the anthropometric data given here are weighted toward United States Air Force personnel; the results of other studies have differed slightly.)

Symbol		Location on figure		
		Coordinates - - %height		
		X	Y	Z
	Hinge Points			
A	Base of skull on spine	0.0	0.0	91.23
B	Shoulder joint	0.0	±10.66	81.16
C	Elbow	0.0	±10.66	62.20
D	Hip	0.0	± 5.04	52.13
E	Wrist	0.0	±10.66	46.21
F	Knee	0.0	± 5.04	28.44
G	Ankle	0.0	± 5.04	3.85
	Centres of gravity			
1	Head	0.0	0.0	93.48
2	Trunk-Neck	0.0	0.0	71.09
3	Upper-Arm	0.0	±10.66	71.74
4	Lower Arm	0.0	±10.66	55.33
5	Hand	0.0	±10.66	43.13
6	Upper Leg	0.0	± 5.04	42.48
7	Lower Leg	0.0	± 5.04	18.19
8	Foot	3.85	± 6.16	1.78
S	Total (whole body)			55.27

Weight Distribution of the human body
Percent of total body weight
6.9
46.1
6.6
4.2
1.7
21.5
9.6
3.4
100.00

Figure 40

(From the *Bioastronautics Data Book*, National Aeronautics and Space Administration, Washington).

Each part has its own Centre of Gravity, lying fairly exactly along the longitudinal axis, always nearer the proximal joint (i.e. the joint nearer the trunk). The tables show the relative *average masses* (average, since these vary in individuals) of different parts of the body, taking the total mass of the body as 100 per cent.

Here, in an erect position with arms to sides, a man's Centre of Gravity (S) averages 55·27 per cent of his height, approximately 1½ inches below the navel, roughly midway between the belly and the back.

Children will average a relatively higher Centre of Gravity in such a position, owing to carrying relatively more weight in their upper body. But, again on average, a woman's Centre of Gravity in this position will be slightly lower, relative to her height, because of her smaller thorax, lighter arms and narrower shoulders, but heavier pelvis and thighs and shorter legs. But the Centre of Gravity lies higher in the trunk of shorter-legged women than in longer-legged males with correspondingly short trunks—an important point when considering the performances of women in high-jumping, hurdling, the running events and in some gymnastic exercises where the body is supported completely by the arms.

The location of the Centre of Gravity for any particular person, in any given position, changes with inspiration and expiration, upon eating and drinking and with an increase of fat or age.

For our later observations it will be important to know only the approximate position of this point, and to appreciate that it moves always in sympathy with the movements of the different parts of the body. It is, in fact, a most unstable point in the athlete, and yet, despite its almost continuous motion, it seldom leaves the pelvic cavity.

Motion in contact with the ground. By moving when in contact with the ground an athlete changes the position of his Centre of Gravity both in relation to his mass and to the ground itself. And this applies whether he is in *direct* contact (as, for example, when he is actually touching the ground) or indirect contact (as in pole vaulting, when he is in the air, but holding the pole).

To give examples: if, from the standing position of Fig. 40 he raises his right arm horizontally to the side (Fig. 41*a*) his Centre of Gravity shifts to his right and is raised about 1¼ in.; and when the other arm is stretched out similarly (Fig. 41*b*) the Centre of Gravity rises by the same amount again but returns to the body's centre-line.

Then, when both arms are raised directly overhead (Fig. 41*c*) it moves an additional 2½ in. higher in the trunk. (In Fig. 41 these move-

Figure 41   a   b   c

ments of the Centre of Gravity have been purposely exaggerated.) In a crouch starting position (Fig. 42) an athlete's Centre of Gravity is

Figure 42   *Figure 43*

lower and brought well forward of the feet, and a pole vaulter who drops his legs while clearing the cross-bar also lowers his Centre of Gravity (if no other movement is involved) while he holds the pole.

In exceptional forms of movement, however, this point can lie *outside* the body. In the position shown in Fig. 43 the Centre of Gravity might be as much as 3 in. outside and below the stomach (varying according to the build and flexibility of the athlete). Variations of this 'piked' or 'jacked' position are sometimes used in pole vaulting, long-jumping, diving, etc.

Motion in the air. We have already seen (page 120) that once an athlete

55

Figure 44

breaks contact with the ground the flight curve of his Centre of Gravity is smooth and undisturbed until contact is regained. Certainly no movement of the athlete while off the ground interrupts it.

As an extreme example of this we can take the exploding of a shrapnel shell in the air (Fig. 44). Air resistance apart, the shell's Centre of Gravity describes a smooth curve both *before* and *after* the mid-air explosion, until fragments of it strike other objects. The force of its explosion, working in all directions, leaves the path of its Centre of Gravity unchanged.

This principle of the maintenance of the path of the Centre of Gravity

Figure 45

is exemplified in the hitch-kick (i.e. running-in-the-air) style in long-jumping (Fig. 147) where the athlete cannot alter the flight path of his Centre of Gravity although, for other reasons, his movements have their value (see pages 111 and 170–2).

If the long-jumper were permitted to carry weights, he *could* gain additional height and speed by throwing them down and back in the air; for, through the two-way action of force, the impulse so derived would also influence his body, but in an opposite direction—the tech-

Figure 46   a

nique used by the professional athletes of nineteenth-century England, some of whom long-jumped more than 30 ft.*

(It is interesting to note that in ancient Greek times when weights (*halteres*) *were* used in jumping for distance, they were *not* released in the air but, with the arms, were swung back prior to the landing. Thus the weights were used only to improve the take-off impulse and advance the jumper's heels in relation to the combined Centre of Gravity of athlete and halteres.)

The modern jumper's movements in the air, therefore, alter his body position only in relation to his Centre of Gravity; they cannot jet-propel him. When in the air, a part of his body moves one way, some other part moves in an opposite direction, simultaneously, so that the product of masses and distances about the Centre of Gravity is unchanged. If, for example, the head and feet move down (as in a dive straddle (Fig. 45) then the hips are made to move up.

But it should be noted that the reaction to a movement in the air need not comprise the units of mass and distance which caused it; e.g. when, using a Western Roll (Fig. 46a), a high-jumper reaches towards the pit with his inside arm the simultaneous reaction can be that of a fractional raising of the rest of the body mass (Fig. 46b) or, to take the other extreme, a pronounced lifting of an even lighter part of the athlete. We see from Fig. 46c that when the arm action is accompanied by a raising of the other arm, the trunk and hips gain no additional height in relation to the Centre of Gravity; one movement cancels out the beneficial effect of the other. Under such circumstances, therefore, it is important which part of the athlete absorbs the reaction.

* However, the discarding of the weights has no effect on the motion of the *common* Centre of Gravity of the system, i.e. weights and athlete combined.

b   c

Friction

Friction occurs when one body moves, or tries to move, in contact with another hindering or opposing motion. The measure of frictional resistance is the force necessary to maintain a body's uniform motion. In track and field athletics the term *'friction'* is often used in connection with the movement of the feet on the ground, when frictional force varies with the nature of the ground and shoe surfaces, the force pushing them together, and the relative motion between them.

Surprisingly, perhaps, the area of contact, e.g. the size of the shoe, is unimportant. A small shoe, in comparison with a larger one, reduces the area of contact but, other things being equal, the force pushing it against the ground is greater per unit area. These two effects cancel out each other; frictional force is the same in both cases.

If there were no such thing as friction athletes could not run, jump or throw, but could merely raise or lower their body weight; for the performance of all these activities is partly dependent upon horizontally-directed thrusts against the ground evoking ground reactions of equal magnitude in opposite directions. A sprinter wearing frictionless ball-bearings under his shoes on smooth ice, could not move his Centre of Gravity in any horizontal direction—for even a fraction of an inch.

These considerations apply to athletes wearing plimsolls, basketball boots, etc. (as in shot putting, discus throwing and hammer throwing); but in other events (e.g. sprinting, hurdling, javelin throwing, jumping) an athlete cannot get sufficient horizontal thrust without the use of spikes which, provided the surface of the track is firm, enable him to exert a large thrust against the ground without any horizontal movement of his foot.

Friction will oppose the runner when his foot meets the ground at a speed relative to his Centre of Gravity in a backward direction, which is less than the Centre of Gravity's forward speed over the ground. To illustrate, if the sprinter in Fig. 47a is travelling at twenty miles an hour and, relative to his Centre of Gravity, his foot moves back at nineteen miles an hour as it contacts the track—then the foot, relative to the ground, moves *forward* at one mile an hour, braking his forward motion. This happens sometimes when an athlete overstrides.

On the other hand, in Fig. 47b, where the foot is moving back at twenty-two miles an hour (for the same twenty-mile-per-hour body speed), the limb, correctly, drives the body instead of the body driving the limb. Continued acceleration and the maintenance of top sprinting speed largely depend upon the ability to oscillate the limbs rapidly in

Figure 47   a   b

order to obtain this essential foot speed; at maximum sprinting speed, however, there is little relative movement between foot and ground when touch-down occurs.

It must be pointed out that there are great losses of energy within the human machine due to internal friction. However, this is mainly a physiological question and does not enter into a consideration of external forces acting on the human body.

Equilibrium* or balance

Correct balance—at rest and in motion—is a vital factor in athletic events, and must often be achieved under difficult circumstances.

Balance and stability at rest. The first consideration for balance (or equilibrium, as it is called in mechanics) is that the resultant of all the forces acting on the object shall be zero. To take the simple examples in Fig. 48: in both resting positions the force of gravity pulling the brick down is equal but opposite to that of the ground pushing it up. Under such conditions —and this applies to all athletes balanced at rest, too—a plumb-line

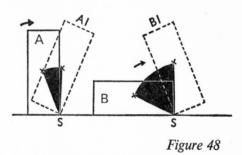

Figure 48

dropped from the Centre of Gravity falls within the base.

* From Latin words meaning 'equal weights'. The expression is applied to the condition where the effects of forces on a system cancel out, leaving the system unchanged.

Balanced objects, however, possess varying degrees of firmness or steadiness in their positions; their *stability* varies. We can see at once that it is easier to upset the brick towards the right in position (*a*) than in (*b*); to do this the Centre of Gravity, marked X, must pass over and beyond the far edges, the *angle* through which it must tilt to lose balance in (*a*) being considerably less than in (*b*); less *work* is performed, too, in raising the Centre of Gravity. And the required horizontal *force*, acting through the Centre of Gravity, is also less. But a heavier brick would be more stable in both positions; it would take more work and more force to topple it.

It follows, therefore, that an object's stability depends upon:

The area of its base

The height of its Centre of Gravity

The horizontal distance between the Centre of Gravity and the pivoting edge

Its weight

Figs 42 and 49 exemplify the application of these principles to athletics. To be steady on his marks (as the rules demand) the sprinter adopts a position where his base is long and fairly broad (Fig. 42), with the Centre of Gravity above it. But for a quick, forceful getaway he crouches with his Centre of Gravity as high and as far forward as circumstances permit; his stability is not great.

On the other hand, an initial position for a standing put (Fig. 49*a*) is much more stable in a forward direction. The base (which includes not only the feet, but also the intervening area) is wider and the Centre of Gravity (common to both man and shot) comparatively far away from the eventual pivot, the front foot. But a plumb-line dropped from his Centre of Gravity falls within the base, as with the sprinter.

The athlete of Fig. 49*b* is also balanced, but balanced precariously

Figure 49

a   b

Figure 50

on one foot. To improve stability and avoid fouling he flexes the supporting leg and lowers his trunk, thus lowering his Centre of Gravity. Body mass outside the base does not upset balance unless it alters the position of the athlete's Centre of Gravity.

The standing starting position (Fig. 50) is certainly more stable than the thrower's of Fig. 49*b*, but in comparison to a crouched stance (Fig. 42) the base is too narrow and short, and the Centre of Gravity too high—which accounts for the 'rolling' starts seen so often in distance running. In all these positions a heavier athlete, equal in all other respects, will have greater stability.

Although a balanced position is more difficult to attain the higher the Centre of Gravity, the *correction* of balance will be easier—because the speed of the Centre of Gravity will develop less quickly the greater its distance above the base. Thus, a knife is more easily balanced point downward, by moving the finger, than point upward. But for a *stationary* balanced position the point of the knife should be uppermost.

Balance in motion. Let us consider, for the present, balance in motion to mean that, as a whole, an object or athlete is moving without rotation.

In Fig. 51*a* a stick is balanced upright in the palm of a hand. When the hand moves forward (Fig. 51*b*) force is applied to the bottom of the stick, causing it to rotate backward. On a second attempt, however, the stick is tilted forward as the hand accelerates (Fig. 51*c*). The force of the stick's weight, acting through the Centre of Gravity (now outside the base), tends to rotate it forward, and if the stick leans neither too much nor too little for the force applied by the hand it remains balanced. *Thus, clockwise and counter-clockwise rotations cancel out—the second condition for equilibrium.*

Figure 51

When force ceases to be exerted and the motion of stick and hand is therefore uniform, the stick must be upright again to stay in balance (Fig. 51*a*). Or, if its speed is such by now that air resistance is sufficiently strong, it must lean forward just enough to offset the force of the air.

When the hand applies a braking force, the tendency will be for the stick to fall forward. Now, to stay balanced, it must lean backward (Fig. 51*d*), and the greater the retarding force the greater this backward lean must be. Finally to remain balanced when the hand is no longer moving, the stick must be upright again (Fig. 51*a*).

This simple example illustrates an important aspect of the interplay of forces in the maintenance of balance in motion. To take an example from athletics, Fig. 52 depicts a runner's final position in driving his body forward. The reaction to the force of his drive against the ground (here, for simplicity, assumed to pass through his Centre of Gravity) is divided into its forward (F1) and upward (F2) components, which tend respectively to rotate the athlete backward and forward. To run with balance (ignoring air resistance) the force turning him forward at this instant of the stride cycle must exactly counteract the force rotating backward. For balance, any alteration of one of these forces requires an adjustment in the other.

Again, at the start of a sprint the athlete's effective horizontal driving force is much greater than in our previous illustration, for it is easier to push backward with full force against the ground; the tendency to rotate backward is therefore greater. Now, for balanced running the turning effect of the force of the upward component of drive is increased

Figure 52

Figure 53

by working at a greater horizontal distance from the Centre of Gravity (Fig. 53). (This principle will be more fully discussed in Chapter Five under *Moments* (page 64) and *Running*, pages 128–32.)

Balance in the air—of particular importance to jumpers, vaulters, hurdlers, divers and gymnasts—will be discussed under *Angular Motion* in Chapter Five (page 111).

Angular Motion

Most of the movement in track and field athletics is of an angular character because the human body, mechanically speaking, comprises a system of levers capable only of rotational motion. And what at first sight often appears to be linear movement is, on analysis, found to be the end product of a series of complex rotations of many parts of the body. It is therefore important, in analysing athletic technique, to be familiar with the principles governing rotational motion.

Moments

It is easier to hold a javelin in a horizontal position at its point of balance (i.e. at its Centre of Gravity) (Fig. 54a) than farther down the

Figure 54

shaft, and most difficult of all (if not impossible!) to keep it in this position while grasping the tail end (Fig. 54*b*).

And yet the javelin weighs no more, and the person holding it does not get progressively weaker! The increasing difficulty is due to the tendency for the javelin to rotate—a tendency which grows with an increase in horizontal distance between the force of its weight, acting through the Centre of Gravity, and the hand.

The following are dynamic examples of the same phenomenon; wheels, revolving doors and propellers are easier to turn when force is applied as far away as possible from their axes—the hub, hinge or shaft. A heavy door is progressively easier to close as one pushes farther and farther away from its hinges.

These illustrations indicate that

(i) To turn an object about an axis force must be exerted at a distance from that axis, and the greater the distance, the greater will be the rotational effect. But it is important to note that the distance from the line of action of the force to the axis—the *lever-arm*, as it is called—must be *measured along a perpendicular*, i.e. *at right angles to the direction of the force*. (See Fig. 55.)

(ii) A larger force will produce a greater turning effect.

The product of the force and the lever-arm is called the *moment of the force*, or *torque**, and is used as a measure of this turning effect; and the product of torque and the time for which it acts is known as the *angular impulse*.

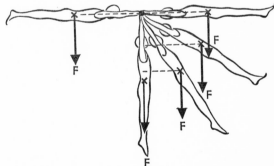

Figure 55

Horizontal bar exercises. The turning effect of the force of gravity on the swinging gymnast is greater when his body is horizontal, and diminishes progressively as he assumes a more vertical position. Obviously, a change in body position during the swing also increases or decreases the lever arm and influences swinging speed.

* From the Latin word, meaning 'to twist'.

Moments in equilibrium. In both horizontal positions (Fig. 54) the javelin is in equilibrium, because, first, the resultant of all the forces acting on it is zero and, second, clockwise and counter-clockwise moments cancel each other out. It will help to study this in greater detail.

In Fig. 54a the hand merely exerts an upward force of 1 lb 12¼ oz—equal to the javelin's weight. But in the other position (Fig. 54b) this force by itself will not produce equilibrium, even though the sum of the forces is zero. We must refer to the second condition for equilibrium and take the moments into account.

In this position three forces act on the javelin: (1) the forefinger, acting as the axis or fulcrum, exerts an upward force; (2) the javelin's weight, which has a clockwise moment about this finger; and (3) the downward force exerted by the thumb, which has a counter-clockwise moment. These two moments cancel out each other.

If we assume the lever-arm of the weight's force to be 3 ft, then its clockwise moment will be 1 lb 12¼ oz × 3. And if the thumb presses down 3 in. away from the fulcrum—i.e. $\frac{1}{12}$th of the distance of the weight's lever-arm—then, for equilibrium, it must exert 12 times more

units of force (12 × 1 lb 12¼ oz = 21 lb 3 oz).

As the sum of all the forces must be zero, the two downward forces (1 lb 12¼ oz and 21 lb 3 oz) must equal the forefinger's upward pressure of 22 lb 15¼ oz. So the hand exerts two forces; an upward one of 22 lb 15¼ oz and a downward one of 21 lb 3 oz. It is hardly surprising that the javelin is more difficult to hold in this position!

From the first position in which the javelin was held (Fig. 54a) it can be seen that an object's or athlete's Centre of Gravity is actually a point where the combined moments of the many separate gravitational pulls on all the particles of mass on one side, acting clockwise, equal the combined counter-clockwise moments on the other. (See also page 52.)

Whenever, at rest, a plumb-line can be dropped from the Centre of Gravity to fall within the base (i.e. the hand in Fig. 54a) the various turning effects automatically cancel out—as with the bricks (Fig. 48) and the balanced athletes (Figs. 52 and 53).

Balance in acceleration can be maintained by altering the position of the body, thus shifting the Centre of Gravity so as to lengthen or shorten the lever-arms of the component forces applied. For example, the stick in Fig. 56 remains balanced during linear acceleration when the product of upward force-component and its horizontal distance to the Centre of Gravity is equal to that of the forward component and its distance vertically to the Centre of Gravity.

Figure 56

When the stick leans in the direction of the acceleration its Centre of Gravity is lowered, reducing the lever-arm of the horizontal component of drive and the backward-rotating effect it encourages. Simultaneously, the lever-arm of the vertical component is increased, as is the tendency to rotate the stick forward (Fig. 56).

It follows that a sprinter who leans forward too much for the effective force of his leg drive totters, unbalanced, from his marks. Or if he is too upright his legs will seem to move ahead of him and lose their driving effect; this can also happen when a distance runner, surprised by an unexpected challenge, responds without making the necessary adjustment to his body lean.

In efficient running the ratio of forward to upward component of the reaction to leg drive influences the angle of the trunk. At the start, where it is easy to push forcefully backward against the ground, the sprinter needs a pronounced forward lean, but as his speed increases so will the effective force of his drive be reduced, necessitating a progressive modification towards a more erect position. Again, a bounding type of runner, using a comparatively greater vertical drive component may need a more upright carriage to shorten the lever-arm of the force and so reduce the tendency to rotate forward.

It is quite possible for athletes who enjoy exceptional hip mobility and who possess certain postural characteristics to make the necessary adjustments to the position of the Centre of Gravity without employing the more orthodox forward trunk lean—hence their comparatively upright running positions even during acceleration. The great Jesse Owens and E. McDonald Bailey spring readily to mind as good examples of this (see also pages 128–32).

Problems of balance in running and jumping during those phases in which athletes are in contact with the ground are best considered, as in our previous examples, by taking moments about the Centre of Gravity, not the point of support. For, in dealing with the body as a whole, movement on the ground in these events is the combination of a series of linear accelerations whereby clockwise and counter-clockwise turning moments about the point of support cannot be equal.

But if an athlete is balanced in motion, *in the sense that there is no turning of the whole body mass,* moments about his Centre of Gravity may be considered equal. (See also page 129.) As a general principle it is usually more convenient to consider an axis passing through the Centre of Gravity in all events where, subsequently, the athlete leaves the ground.

However, in analysing balance in pole vaulting and throwing positions (where the athlete has contact with the ground) it is sometimes convenient to take moments about the base or support, thinking in terms of *turning couples.* We use a couple when winding a clock or manipulating a corkscrew. Examples follow.

A hammer thrower's equilibrium in a saggittal plane is partly the result of two pairs of parallel, equal, forces acting in opposite directions (Fig. 57a)* The hammer's centrifugal pull and the equal force of the ground thrusting at an angle against the thrower's feet form one couple tending to rotate him counter-clockwise; the distance at right angles to the line of these parallel forces is the *arm* of the couple.

In a clockwise direction, however, the force of the thrower's weight, acting downward through his Centre of Gravity, plus the equal but upward force of the ground under his feet, form a second couple, the arm of which is the horizontal distance between the lines of these two vertically directed forces (Fig. 57a).

Again, a pole vaulter's rotation over the crossbar is due, mainly, to a couple created by the reaction to his thrust on the pole, acting vertically

Figure 57

* For simplicity, the hammer's weight and the centrifugal forces of the thrower's body have not been considered.

upwards, and the force of his weight, pulling vertically downwards (Fig. 57*b*). The turning moment of a couple is found by multiplying *one* of its forces (*it should be noted that they are always equal in size*) by its arm.

Moments in rotation and spin. Just as, with linear acceleration, moments about the support cannot be equal, so it is with angular acceleration, whether the axis is considered to be a point of contact with the ground or the Centre of Gravity.

In analysing a diver's movements (Fig. 58) we take moments about his Centre of Gravity. When the reaction to his leg thrust (along a straight line drawn between foot and hip) passes directly through his Centre of Gravity, pure translatory motion occurs, i.e. he leaves the board without rotation (Fig. 58*a*). But as, in successive dives (Fig. 58*b* and *c*) he exerts a force at increasing horizontal distances to his Centre of Gravity, the effect is as though more is used progressively in imparting a rotation, while less is available to project his body.

In fact, a *given reaction* (*i.e. vertical impulse*) *to leg thrust will impart the same vertical speed, and therefore the same height, to a diver's body, whether directed through his Centre of Gravity or not* (see page 27). But here (Fig. 58*b* and *c*) the difficulty is to exert the same impulse (i.e. force x time) as previously (Fig. 58*a*) *against a rotating body.*

To achieve the same height the diver in Fig. 58*b* would have to develop *a greater thrust from the board*; greater still for the rotation

Figure 58

of Fig. 58*c*. In both cases the leg-thrust would need to be faster, reducing the *time* of operation and, consequently, requiring greater thrust. (See pages 36–8.)

If a body is turning in an *opposite* direction to that in which it will finally be made to rotate by an eccentric thrust, that thrust will be more effective in driving the body linearly, since it will be doing this while it is reducing the turn to zero. This could be one of the advantages to be derived from a 'rolling' start in sprinting (which, of course, is not permitted by the rules). It could result in the application of a greater horizontal component of force. The contrary twisting of hips and shoulders in running is another example. (See also pages 125–8.)

Eccentric thrusts, as shown in Fig. 58*b* and *c*, are wasteful of energy. Assuming, for the moment, that the diver in Fig. 58 projects his Centre of Gravity to the same height in all three dives; in Fig. 57*a* the point of application of the thrust moves through the same distance and acquires the same velocity as his Centre of Gravity; but when the same take-off impulse is directed eccentrically (Fig. 58*b* and *c*) this point moves through a greater distance than his Centre of Gravity.

As the expenditure of energy is measured by the work done (see page 43) this in Fig. 57*b* is greater than in Fig. 58*a*—and even more so in Fig. 58*c*. Thus, an impulse exerted through the Centre of Gravity changes a body's linear kinetic energy while an equal impulse exerted 'off centre' changes the body's linear kinetic energy by the same amount, *but also* imparts rotational kinetic energy. Hence, unless rotation is required, eccentric thrust is wasteful of energy.

The diver's rotation off the board is brought about, in fact, by a turning couple; the reaction to his leg thrust, i.e. the force of the springboard, acts vertically upward and the force of his weight, acting through his Centre of Gravity, pulls vertically downward. He obtains this eccentric or sideways thrust about the Centre of Gravity by bringing his head and arms (i.e. just under a fifth of his total body mass) forward

Figure 59

beforehand and, in bad diving, by bending forward markedly from his hips (Fig. 59).

We have seen that the forces of a couple must be equal and yet, in diving from the springboard, the force of the upward vertical thrust actually exceeds the downward pull on the man's body. The forces turning him are indeed equal, but it is the excess of force from the board which projects him into the air. If his Centre of Gravity moved downward, i.e. he fell off the board, then the reverse would apply: the force of his body weight would then be greater than that which passed through his feet.

As Orner* has written, 'If a competitor performs a well-executed dive, it will be good because the direction, height and the force of rotation imparted to his body through the diving-board are a close approximation to his exact needs for the correct number of somersaults in the particular position intended and his control in the air will be quite marginal.

'The picture of a diver jumping from the board steeply without rotation then circling deliberately for a spin, finally halting his rotation completely to dart vertically into the water is pure illusion—and the diver's art! The illusion is most effectively shattered when a diver errs on take-off by taking too much turning force, and is unable to maintain the impression of "stopped" rotation near the water.

'Unfortunately, many divers and coaches believe in the possibility of controlling dives fully in the air and are taken in by the illusion. The inevitable result is that they concern themselves mainly with the dive; that is the effects, rather than with the take-off in which errors showing in the dive originate in a proportion of at least 90 per cent.'

Levers

The muscle forces of the human body are applied through a system of levers (bones rotating about their joints) to which the principle of moments, discussed earlier, is fundamental. In analysing movement in sport it is sometimes convenient to regard large segments of an athlete, e.g. an arm, leg or trunk, as a simple lever, in the same way as the use of a piece of apparatus may be analysed in terms of leverage.

The three types of levers (Figs. 60, 65 and 69) are classified according to the arrangement of the *fulcrum* (axis), the *force* and the *resistance*. The fulcra (A) are the joints and through muscle-contraction force is applied at the points where the tendons are attached to the bones (F.)

The resistance (R) may be merely the weight of the lever itself or the combined weight of the lever plus a load, like a shoe or throwing implement (Fig. 62). However, if (and this would be unusual in track and field athletics) the lever acts in a purely horizontal plane, *then the resistance in this plane will be due only to inertia*, resistance to change in motion, the pull of gravity being vertical. This resistance might also be a force acting within, or externally against, the body.

* W. Orner, 'Rebuilding a Champion's armour' (*World Sports*, August 1964).

Figure 60

First class levers. With this type of lever the fulcrum is situated, 'see-saw' fashion, between the applied force and the resistance, both acting in the same direction (Fig. 60). The arms (i.e. the distance between force and fulcrum on the one hand and resistance and fulcrum on the other) may be equal or unequal; but if the force arm is longer the lever will favour effective force, and if it is shorter it will gain in speed and range at the expense of force. Hence 'all that is lost in force is gained in distance, and vice versa'.

Figure 61

Figure 62

In both our examples of first class levers (Figs. 61 and 62) the resistance arm is much longer than the force arm, favouring speed and range but not force. This applies to most levers of the body. If, for example, in Fig. 62 the resistance arm is twelve times longer than the force arm, a triceps force of 96 lb exerts only 8 lb of force on the shot (96 ÷ 12). But such an arrangement has its compensations, since the muscles shorten slowly, thus developing very high tension (see pages 31–2).

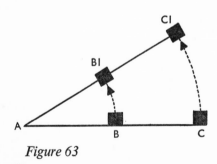

Figure 63

The interdependence of speed and range of action is illustrated in Fig. 63, where a short lever, AB is superimposed on a longer one, AC, both moving with equal angular velocity. The linear velocity of the lever ends is proportional to their radii; therefore, if AC is twice as long as AB, its end will travel twice the distance in a given time, i.e. it will have twice the linear velocity.

Fig. 64 shows another first class lever, where a heavy stone is raised by means of a crowbar, and, to take an example from athletics, when a pole vaulter adopts the 'carry' position, the downward force he has to exert with his rear hand is many times greater than the force of gravity pulling on the pole in front of his other hand, the fulcrum.

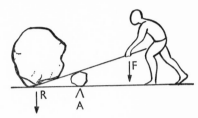

Figure 64

Second class levers. With levers of this class both force and resistance act on the same side of the fulcrum, but in opposite directions and with a longer force arm (Fig. 65). It therefore favours force, at the expense of speed and range: a wheelbarrow is another example of a second class lever (Fig. 66). But levers of this type are not common in track and field athletics.

Figure 65

The foot is used as a second class lever when a person rises on the toes (Fig. 67). When the calf muscles pull on the heels, the body rises. Thus the toes become the fulcrum and the body weight lies between it and the point where force is applied, i.e. the heels, providing one of the few instances where the body's musculature works at a mechanical advantage. (If the applied force is vertically upward it will evoke a

Figure 66

Figure 67

73

Figure 68

vertically downward reaction which must be added to body weight and be supported by the toes). (See also pages 28–30, Newton's Third Law.)

This is exemplified in progressively loading the calf muscles by rising on the toes, with weights (Fig. 68). In this particular exercise the pull of the calf muscles through the heel bone (with the toes as the fixed point) enables a relatively large load to be manipulated easily; for the line of action (through the common Centre of Gravity of body and barbell) is arranged so that it falls close to the fulcrum, viz. the toes (Fig. 68*b*).

The closer this line is to the fulcrum, the shorter is the weight arm and the smaller the muscular force required in lifting, and vice versa.

Figure 69

Figure 70

The technique of weight *lifting* (where the aim is to lift the heaviest possible load) therefore requires that the weight arm shall be as short as possible; while the weight *trainer* (who is primarily concerned with the strengthening effect of the exercise) might attempt to lengthen it, *although this could lead to an unstable and even dangerous position.**

However, when in the exercise (Fig. 68*b*) the person leans forward sufficiently to move the common Centre of Gravity *in front of* the toes, or when the toes and heel are free to move around the ankle joint (Fig. 61) the calf muscles can then operate the foot as a first class lever. This illustrates how the levers of the body can sometimes be used in more than one way; how, by a change in position, fulcra and points of resistance can be altered. (The muscular effect of this exercise is doubled, of course, when the full body weight is taken by only one leg).

Third class levers. These are by far the most common of body levers. Here the fulcrum is at one end and the resistance at the other, with the force in between. Force and resistance work in opposing directions (Fig. 69). Third class levers lack great force of action. When, for example, a 16 lb shot is supported in the hand (Fig. 70*b*), the flexor muscles of the upper arm must exert a force of about 160 lb, because the force arm is approximately ten times shorter than the resistance arm. Most of the muscles of the body are inserted near the joint in this fashion,

Figure 71

with the resistance at the far end of the bone lever. A weak, long-levered athlete is therefore at a distinct disadvantage, for he can employ his levers against only very light resistances.

Examples of third class leverage are numerous in athletics. Taking, as illustration, movement in the horizontal plane: in the delivery phases of all the throwing events, force is applied between the athlete's fulcrum (i.e. his axis) and the resistance (the implement) (Fig. 71).

* G. T. Adamson, 'Some facts and fallacies on fitness training' (A.A.A. Coaching Newsletter No. 15, July 1960, Amateur Athletic Association, England), page 3.

Because of the short lever-arm such movements require great force of muscle action, even where the missile is comparatively light.

Force arms and resistance arms can alter with body movement; e.g. Fig. 70 (*a* and *b*) illustrate how, with the humerus held in a vertical position, both arms increase as the elbow bends—keeping the ratio between them (and, therefore, the degree of lifting difficulty) approximately constant. Again, when the forearm is raised from the horizontal (Fig. 70*c*) both force arm and resistance arm decrease.

In discussing the three classes of lever it has been convenient to assume that force is always applied at right angles, but in the action of muscles on the bone levers this is the exception rather than the rule. In fact, many muscles of the body never pull at an angle exceeding 20 deg.

The more acute the angle of muscle-pull, the farther and faster will a given degree of contraction move the bone, but this, again, is balanced by loss of effective force. Resolving the muscle-pull into two component forces: one, acting at right angles to the bone lever, is beneficial, moving the lever about its fulcrum, the joint (Fig. 72); but the other, acting along the line of the lever towards the joint, stabilises the joint by increasing friction, but makes no contribution to lever motion (Fig. 72). Usually, the stabilising component is much larger than the rotary component. Under these circumstances it is fortunate, indeed, that muscles exert their maximum force when stretched, pulling at acute angles.

There is, therefore, an important distinction between mere force of muscle, and strength, which takes the application of force, leverage, also

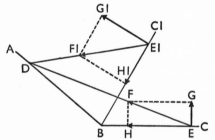

Figure 72

(From *Kinesiology and Applied Anatomy*, by Philip J. Rasch, Ph.D., and Roger K. Burke, Ph.D. (Henry Kimpton))

In Fig. 72, the line AB represents a stationary bone, and BC a moving one. When the muscle DE pulls at an angle DEB, the force contributing to motion (as represented by the line EG) is considerably less than when the bone lever is moved to BC1, where the effective force is represented by the line E1G1. This is because as the muscle's angle of pull changes, so do the sides of the parallelogram.

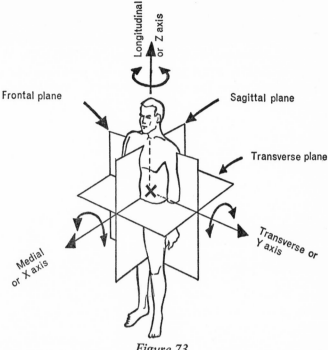

Figure 73

In an erect posture the longitudinal (Z) axis is vertical and the medial (X) and transverse (Y) axes are horizontal ; but all three can have their positions relative to the ground changed with a change in body-attitude (see page 90). Where an athlete is in contact with the ground he may often be considered to rotate about axes parallel to those shown.

into account. Some athletes, fortunately endowed, possess muscular insertions that are farther from their joints than in the average person; and this, if true of one of their bone levers, appears to apply to them all! Only a very small difference is necessary to give considerable mechanical advantage.

Axes

The axis of a revolving body is a straight line, itself at rest in the body, about which all other parts rotate in a plane at right angles. We know that different parts of an athlete have their own axes, the joints, but here we shall consider the revolution of the *whole body mass*. Fig. 73 illustrates the principal axes of rotation, and planes, of the human body in a normal standing position—with the mutually perpendicular axes passing through its Centre of Gravity.

Axes when in contact with the ground. There are countless instances in sport where athletes revolve in a vertical or near vertical plane about *para*-medial or *para*-transverse axes through their points of support. In a cartwheel, for example (Fig. 74), the gymnast turns about his hands and then about his feet—i.e. about a para-medial axis.

| Figure 74 | Figure 75 | Figure 76 |

Likewise, take-off movements in long jumping (Fig. 147*a* and *b*) and the pivoting of the body on the supporting foot in running (Fig. 126*d–f*) can be thought of as rotations of the whole body about a para-transverse axis at a point where the foot meets the ground. Again, a pole vaulter (Fig. 153) swings about his hands immediately after take-off, or he and his pole, combined, can be thought of as a mass rotating about a para-transverse axis where the pole contacts the box—also applicable to a gymnast swinging by his hands on a horizontal bar (Fig. 55).

Nor need the extremities always be the point of support although, in track and field athletics, this is most common. In certain gymnastic exercises, for example, it is the head (in a headspring, Fig. 75), the shoulders (in a neckspring, Fig. 76), or the back or buttocks, as in certain tumbling movements.

Motion about a vertical or near-vertical axis is equally common in sport; and in track and field athletics the discus and hammer throwing events are good examples.

With rotations of this type the body's axis passes through (a) the base of support and (b) a point determined by the balancing about that base of the clockwise and counter-clockwise moments of *weight* and *centrifugal forces.* (Fig. 77).

When the athlete's posture is *symmetrical* (i.e. his or her position on one side is a mirrored image of the position on the opposite side)

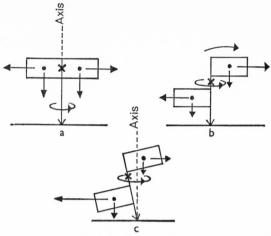

Figure 77

Fig. 77 is a simplified model representing an athlete twisting about a vertical axis.
(a) The two identical rectangular blocks are set symmetrically in relation to the point of support and, therefore, their clockwise and counter-clockwise moments of weight and centrifugal force about the base balance. A stable condition is achieved temporarily, and the axis of rotation passes through the model's Centre of Gravity.
(b) With one block now lower than the other, their weights balance about the base but their moments of centrifugal force do not. The position is unstable.
(c) For balance, now, the figure must be tilted to equalise all moments about the base (corresponding to a change of posture in a rotating athlete); and a frictional force must be introduced there. In consequence, the figure's Centre of Gravity and its vertical axis will not coincide and the figure will remain unstable, requiring a continual shifting of its base.

this axis will always pass through the point of support and the common Centre of Gravity (which includes clothing worn and any apparatus carried).

In the position shown in Fig. 78, therefore, the skater pirouettes about an axis which passes through the point of the skate in contact with the ice and, also, very close to her Centre of Gravity; for her position may be considered approximately symmetrical.

But where the position is markedly *asymmetrical* (as in the case of the rotating hammer thrower, Fig. 85) the axis, although still passing through the base, will not necessarily pass through the Centre of Gravity and the position will be markedly unstable.

In those activities (as in the shot, hammer, javelin and discus events) where some turning movements are made with both feet in contact with the ground, the support or base includes both feet and the inter-

Figure 78

vening ground; so, in such cases, an axis can actually fall between the feet and move (as it must, in good throwing) from one point of the base to another (Fig. 79).

Most athletic events combine turning movements about both types of axes.

Axes in the air. For the purpose of analysing the movement of a body (e.g. an athlete or throwing implement) in the air (i.e. without contact with the ground, direct or indirect) it is convenient to consider the rotation about an *axis of momentum* passing through the Centre of Gravity, because of the regularity of that point's flight path. The position of this axis relative to the ground depends upon turning movement (i.e. angular impulse) imparted to the body prior to breaking contact, but, unlike the body's principal axes, *it will remain fixed in direction throughout the jump or dive until contact is regained*, provided air resistance may be disregarded (see also page 89).

Thus, the diver (Fig. 80) rotates about an axis of momentum passing through his Centre of Gravity, and this maintains its direction relative to the ground and water until entry. In the air the high jumper (Fig. 91) turns about an axis of momentum, while his principal axes (Fig. 73) are not fixed in relation to the ground because of his changing attitude in the air. But the axis of momentum of a spinning discus in flight (Fig. 125) can be shifted by air resistance. (See page 119.)

a   b

Figure 79

Figure 80

It is possible for an athlete to turn about this axis of momentum and, simultaneously, about one or a combination of his principal axes—as well as about an *axis of displacement* concerned only with movement originated in flight. But this, and some other aspects of rotational movement in athletics, will be discussed later (see pages 89–119).

A body may sometimes be thought of as having rotation about an axis remote from the body itself. For example, a diver free in space (Fig. 80) can be considered to possess rotation about that point of the springboard where his feet were—a *fixed* axis (see pages 93–4). Again, through correct footwork and other techniques a thrower can increase the missile's radius of motion in turning, so that the path it describes may suggest a *moving* centre of rotation well beyond the circle.

In illustrating principles pertaining to the mechanics of athletics, the concept of a fixed, remote axis is often useful, whereas that of a remote, moving axis is purely academic and of no practical value.

Moment of inertia

We have seen (page 25) that a body's inertia is its resistance to change in motion, and with linear movement mass is the sole measure of that inertia; the greater mass sets up the greater resistance and vice versa.

However, with angular motion the resistance offered to acceleration depends not only upon mass but also upon its distribution about the axis, i.e. the *moment of inertia*; the closer the mass to the axis, the

Figure 81

easier it is to turn. This principle, of great practical application in many problems of human locomotion, explains why one can rotate a limb much more easily about its longitudinal axis than a transverse axis of the same articulation.

In athletics, the distribution of mass can obviously be varied by changing position, by changing shape, about the different axes. For example, flexed or straight, the mass of the arm is the same in both positions in Fig. 81 and yet it is easier to move in the first position (*a*) for there its mass is closer to the shoulder-axis. Its moment of inertia is reduced. Likewise, the flexor muscles which pull the recovery leg forward and upward in running have an easier task with the leg bent than with a greater angle at the knee.

For the same reason the total body mass can be turned more easily about its longitudinal axis than a transverse one, and with most difficulty about a medial axis; all these axes pass through the Centre of Gravity. (Fig. 82). Again, an athlete's resistance to rotation (i.e. his moment of inertia) in pole vaulting is greater with the body extended immediately after take off (Fig. 153*b*) than in the swing-up, where the legs are well flexed (Fig. 153*g*).

To find, accurately, the moment of inertia of the body in any position *about a given axis,** it would be necessary to take each particle separately, multiplying its mass by the square of the distance (measured perpendicularly) to the axis, i.e. its radius; finally, all the separate results should be added together. But since this is obviously not possible, useful if not wholly accurate estimates can be made by using the figures already given (Fig. 40) for the relative average masses of the human body; in estimating the moment of inertia for each of the body units it must be remembered that each separate part has its own Centre of Gravity, lying fairly exactly along a longitudinal line but always slightly nearer the proximal joint (i.e. the joint nearer the trunk).

A person standing rigidly upright on a frictionless turntable with arms extended horizontally (Fig. 83*b*) has, about a vertical axis, approximately three times the moment of inertia of a position where

---

* The body's moment of inertia, unlike its mass, is not inherent to the body, for its value depends on the axis about which is computed.

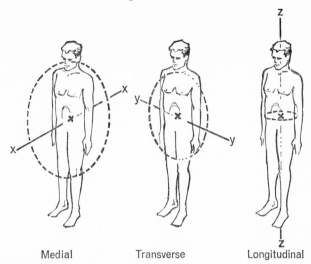

Medial   Transverse   Longitudinal

Figure 82

It is sometimes convenient to imagine the distribution of body mass about a principal axis as a ring (a 'circle of gyration') in which, for the purpose of rotation only, the mass can be considered concentrated—the sum of all the separate moments of inertia of its parts in a particular position. The moment of inertia is then MR^2, where M is the mass and R the 'radius of gyration'.

In an erect posture the moment of inertia of the body is greater about the medial (X) axis than about any other through its Centre of Gravity; least about a longitudinal (Z) axis.

the arms are held to the sides (Fig. 83a). In the first position he is three times more difficult to turn; i.e. to produce an equal angular acceleration, and with the turning force applied at the same point in both positions, the impulse (force × time) must be three times greater; or an equal impulse must be applied at three times the distance to the axis.

In the *arabesque allongé* skating and dancing position (Fig. 83c) resistance to turning will be about six times greater than in Fig. 83a; when the body lies on the table horizontally (Fig. 83d), with the vertical axis passing through its Centre of Gravity, about fourteen times. In fact, relative to an axis passing through its Centre of Gravity, the moment of inertia of the body is least about a longitudinal axis, with the arms extended and close together above the head (Fig. 84a) and greatest when turning in a similar position about a medial axis (Fig. 84b) but with arms parallel. But it is greatest of all in a fully extended position with the hands as axis (Fig. 55) (when, usually, the moment of inertia

83

Figure 83

Figure 84

of the *whole body* is found by adding (1) the moment of inertia of its mass, supposedly concentrated at its Centre of Gravity, about the main axis and (2) its moment of inertia about a parallel axis through its Centre of Gravity). *In fact, the body's moment of inertia is always greater about an axis not passing through its Centre of Gravity than that about a parallel axis that does.*

Angular velocity

The angular velocity of a body moving uniformly is the angle through which it turns in a second. If, for example, an arm moves through a right angle in one second, its angular velocity about the shoulder axis is 90 deg. per second. Likewise, if the somersaulting diver (Fig. 80) turns completely (i.e. through 360 deg.) in two seconds, his angular

Figure 85

velocity will be 180 deg. per second. Angular velocity may also be thought of in terms of revolutions* per second, and there are other units in which it can be measured.

Angular velocities, like velocities, are rarely uniform in athletic movement, but if we wish to determine the angular velocity of a body at a given instant of acceleration, we must assume it to be moving uniformly for a short time; the shorter the period, the more accurate the calculation will be.

When a turning force ceases to act then from Newton's First Law, the body to which it has given velocity will continue to revolve at a uniform rate, or, if brought to rest by force, the body will remain at rest. For example, the diver (Fig. 80) turns in the air as a result of forces applied on the springboard.

It follows, therefore, that an arm or leg can be moving relative to other parts of an athlete's body without force acting simultaneously. However, with the human body, because of internal resistances due to opposing muscle forces and the elastic tensions of fascia, ligaments and tendons, where there is motion of such a kind there is usually force acting also. These internal resistances must always be overcome before force can set the various body levers in motion.

As previously mentioned in connection with levers (page 72), the linear velocity of a point on a turning body is directly proportional to its distance from the axis. Hence (assuming the hammer thrower's hands to be 2ft from the axis passing through his base, and the hammer head 6 ft away) the hands have only one-third of the linear velocity of the hammer (Fig. 85). Again, if two discus throwers turn with equal

* Man can tolerate up to 90 revolutions per minute without undue physiological stress; but for comfort and absence of dizziness five revolutions per minute, or less, seem desirable.

angular velocities, the athlete with the greater radius of discus movement gives greater speed to the missile.

When the body has angular velocity, its motion may be considered as the linear movement of any point, plus a turning about that point with the same angular velocity. For example; the angular velocity with which a long-jumper rotates about his jumping foot as it rests, momentarily, on the board (Fig. 147*a* and *b*) is equal to that with which he can be considered to turn during the take-off about his moving Centre of Gravity; if he does nothing to counteract it before leaving the ground (and maintains this position in the air), it will be the angular velocity with which he will continue to turn about his Centre of Gravity in flight.

The conservation of angular momentum

The product of a turning body's moment of inertia and its angular velocity is called its *angular momentum*, which, like momentum, is a vector quantity possessing both magnitude and direction. *It bears the same relationship to angular impulse as does momentum to impulse* (see pages 36 and 65) and is a concept of the utmost importance in analysing turning movement in sport.

According to the law of the conservation of angular momentum, a turning body isolated from external forces, i.e. left completely by itself, will have a constant angular momentum; that is to say, the product of moment of inertia and angular velocity about the axis of momentum is constant.

If it were possible to make a turntable with frictionless ball-bearings and a man standing on it were set in motion by a push, he would continue for ever to revolve with angular momentum, if we ignore air resistance. By the same token, the angular momenta of divers, high and long-jumpers, etc., whose body masses turn in the air, 'free' in space, may, for all practical purposes, be considered constant in magnitude and direction (for the force of gravity, which acts equally on all parts of a revolving body, can be ignored).

Under these conditions the total angular momentum is entirely unaffected by any rotational movements made with the legs, arms or some other part of an athlete. This will be discussed in more detail later (pages 89–119).

However, by changing the moment of inertia of the body during rotations it is possible, correspondingly, to speed up or slow down the turning rate. If, for example, the man standing on the revolving

86

turntable (Fig. 83*a*) increases his resistance to turning three-fold by stretching his arms sideways (Fig 83*b*), then his angular velocity will be three times slower, and if he resumes his first position (Fig. 83*a*) he will spin at the original rate; but total angular momentum throughout will be unchanged. (See also Appendix, demonstration A.)

The principle is well exemplified in diving. Accepting that, in relation to a horizontal axis passing through the Centre of Gravity, a 'straight' position (Fig. 86*a*) has approximately three and a half times the moment of inertia of a 'tuck' position (Fig. 86*b*), if the diver leaves the springboard with just sufficient angular momentum for a complete somersault in the 'straight' position it will enable him, should he so

Fig. 86 illustrates a geometrical interpretation of angular momentum, taking, as an example, the motion of a diver's ankles around his Centre of Gravity *in a given time*. If the angular momenta of positions a and b are equal, the areas swept out will also be equal. Note the ankle's increase in linear as well as angular velocity in the tucked position. (The angular momentum of a particle about a point is the product of twice the mass and the area swept out in a unit measure of time.)

a b

3½I I

Figure 86

choose, to spin from two to two and a half times 'tucked'. Here allowance is made for the time it takes to adopt the more compact position after leaving the board and a final straightening out prior to entering the water.*

This example from diving points to one way in which turning during flight can be controlled in long-jumping. Should the jumper leave the board rotating forward (as is the general tendency) and then 'jack' or 'tuck' prematurely (as is often the case), his angular velocity is markedly increased thereby and his feet are driven down and back in relation to his Centre of Gravity, for a poor landing. On the other hand, by keeping the body extended in the air, 'jacking' at the last moment, this can be averted (Fig.150). Again, a high-jumper twists quickly in the air when his body's longitudinal axis corresponds closely to his axis of momentum.

Taking another event, a pole vaulter swings slower with his body stretched out just after take-off than when tucked up at the end of the swing, in readiness for his pull-push action.

* Once the surface of the water is broken, the hands or feet become the axis of body rotation. In a good dive, therefore, hands or feet enter just *before* the completion of the required number of somersaults.

Figure 87 a   b   c

Ballet dancers and skaters frequently spin at very high speeds. While they are building up angular momentum their arms are stretched out and the free (non-supporting) leg is permitted to swing wide of the body's vertical axis (Fig. 87a) then, suddenly, the arms and leg are brought in with tremendous effect (Fig. 87b) A graceful finish and slowing down or stopping are then cunningly combined by again extending the arm and free leg masses (Fig. 87c)

Hammer throwers, like the pirouetting dancers and skaters, keep the free leg close to the supporting leg during their turns, thus getting the hips and feet in position quickly, ahead of the rest of the body and the missile.

Figure 89

Figure 88

Again, maintaining balance on ice is the more difficult because of a tendency to rotate (i.e., in a vertical plane), about the body's Centre of Gravity, as opposed to the feet—where, in the latter case, the moment of inertia is greater.

Determining the axis of momentum

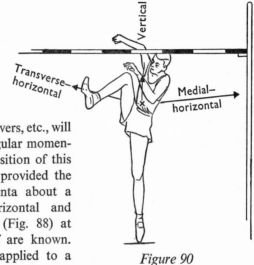

Reference has been made already to an axis of momentum, fixed in direction and about which jumpers, divers, etc., will possess unchanging angular momentum in the air. The position of this axis can be calculated provided the body's separate momenta about a vertical, transverse-horizontal and medial-horizontal axis (Fig. 88) at the instant of take-off are known. Here the principle is applied to a high-jump take-off.

Figure 90

As angular momentum is a vector quantity, each of these three separate turns is represented by a straight line which, in length, is equal

Figure 91

to the magnitude of the corresponding angular momentum; all three meet at the athlete's Centre of Gravity. It has been assumed, for this particular jump, that there is least angular momentum about the vertical axis and most about a medial-horizontal axis; with backward rotation, also, about a transverse-horizontal axis. However, the turning combinations will vary from style to style, and even from one jump to another by the same athlete.

For a resultant to be found, the direction of each separate turn must also be known. Conventionally, positive direction is that which makes the turning look clockwise and, therefore, each axis is looked along so that this is so (Fig 89), and arrow-heads are then added to point accordingly (Fig. 90).

By using the parallelogram method in three dimensions (described in connection with velocity and forces, pages 18 and 39) the magnitude and direction of the total angular momentum and the position of the axis of momentum can then be established. The latter, in the case of our high-jumper, will be slightly at an angle to the horizontal and approximately 45 deg. to the crossbar, fixed in direction throughout the jump (Fig. 91).

In a somersault dive (Fig. 80) or long-jump (Fig. 147) where take-offs are properly balanced, it is not difficult to estimate, from the movements in the air, that the axis of momentum is horizontal. But in many other activities, e.g. high-jumping, it is frequently not perceptible in any but a purely theoretical sense and, in the air, the athlete appears to turn separately, but simultaneously, about his longest and shortest axes; i.e. his axes of minimum and maximum moment of inertia, respectively. In theory it is possible to resolve an athlete's total angular momentum at any time when he is in the air in space—about either the vertical or horizontal axes previously referred to (page 89) which remain fixed in direction, or *his body's* longitudinal, medial and transverse axes, which change their position relative to the ground as the athlete moves in the air. (See also page 114.)

As a matter of interest (for it does not arise in track or field events), given sufficient time the human body moving about a prescribed *fixed* axis will finally settle down to rotate with stable equilibrium, selecting its axis of greatest moment of inertia. This, apart perhaps from a small wobbling called *nutation* (Lat. *nutare*, to nod, see page 117), then coincides with the axis of momentum.

An illustration of this principle can sometimes be seen in the circus or on the variety stage where one performer, suspended from a cord a   b   *Figure 92*

gripped by the teeth, is turned by a partner hanging upside down from a trapeze. At first the suspended person revolves rapidly about the body's long axis (Fig. 92*a*) but quickly (and automatically) assumes a horizontal position, turning about the body's '*preferred*' axis of greatest moment of inertia (Fig. 92*b*).

Turns originating on the ground

A careful analysis of track and field techniques shows that, to greater or lesser degree, almost all athletes break contact with the ground during performance, turning momentarily about an axis of momentum. However, it by no means follows that they are always conscious of it, or should be so.

Imperceptible in good running, it nevertheless occurs on each stride and also during well-executed high-hurdle clearances. More obviously it happens in the jumping events and in the pole vault, as the athlete rotates about the crossbar on releasing the pole.

There are few good hammer throwers whose two feet do not leave the ground, simultaneously, during the last turn, though doubtless this is something not attempted. In all three of the other throwing events, when well performed, the breaking of contact, with a turn in the air, is important at least to the regaining of balance after the throw if not to the throw itself.

Although, as we shall see later, some turns in athletic movement can originate in the air, nevertheless in track and field athletics most are built up while the runner, jumper or thrower is in contact with the ground, when angular momentum can be acquired in the following three ways: *checking linear movement, transference* and *eccentric thrust*. Usually, at least two of these sources are combined.

Checking linear movement. When a body, moving in a straight path,

91

is suddenly checked at an extremity, a *hinged moment* results and angular momentum is developed. For example:

1. In vaulting over a box (Fig. 93) the gymnast, after a preliminary run-up, fixes both feet momentarily at take-off, while the rest of his body rotates over and beyond. This turning continues in the air, bringing the head and shoulders down and feet up in relation to his Centre of Gravity. The clockwise body turn illustrated (Fig. 93) is then reversed when the hands strike the far end.

2. As a result of planting the pole at the end of his approach, the pole vaulter (Fig. 154) rotates simultaneously about his hands and the end of the pole in the box.

3. The diver's somersaults (Fig. 80) can in part be due to checking the feet at take-off on the springboard, as already described.

4. The three previous examples are concerned with angular motion about horizontal axes but, in point of fact, the principle holds for turning about all axes, and sometimes about more than one at a time.

In the javelin event, for example, the thrower checks with his front foot (Fig. 190) and turns, simultaneously, about a horizontal axis (at the point where this foot meets the ground) and a near-vertical axis (passing through the throwing base). This imparts considerable linear velocity to the throwing shoulder and, subsequently, to the javelin. (See also pages 193 and 224–5.)

As the linear movement of a point on a turning body is directly proportional to its distance from the axis, height can be of particular advantage to a thrower. Assuming, for the moment, that after checking with the front foot (Fig 190*e*) the thrower's Centre of Gravity continues at its previous linear velocity, then the shoulder above it must move considerably faster.

However, checking must cause some loss in forward speed and the

Figure 93

more acute the angle between ground and body at the first instant of
contact (or, in the pole vault, the smaller the angle between pole and
ground) the greater the loss will be. The advantage must be weighed
against the disadvantage, as so often in track and field techniques (this
subject is discussed in greater detail in Chapter Ten).

On page 86 it has been stated that an athlete's angular velocity at
take-off is identical about parallel base and Centre of Gravity axes.
However, this must not be taken to mean that the angular momenta
about these axes are also the same; they are not, for the moments of
inertia differ. The angular momentum of the long jumper about a transverse axis through the point where his foot leaves the board is the sum
of two things: (a) angular momentum about the transverse axis through
his Centre of Gravity and (b) the angular momentum of the Centre of
Gravity itself (treated as a massive particle) about the foot. When the

Figure 94　　a　　　　　　　　　　b

Figure 95　　a　　　　　　　　　　b

Figure 96

a   b   c

body leaves the board the second quantity goes on increasing *about the board where the foot was*, because the athlete's weight continues to have a turning moment about this point.* However, the angular momentum about the transverse axis through the Centre of Gravity remains constant for, then, it has no force delivering a turning moment to it.

In analysing athletic techniques it is usually more convenient to consider take-off angular momentum about the Centre of Gravity.

Transference. Momentum, linear or angular, can be transferred from one object to another and from a part of an athlete to his whole body.

An example of the transference of linear momentum is shown in Fig. 94. If a snooker ball, rolling without 'side'† strikes one end of a row of balls, its momentum is transferred to the ball at the far end; if two balls are used (Fig. 95) then, on impact, two balls roll at the other end.

Transference of angular momentum from a part to the whole of the human body can be simply demonstrated (Fig. 96). From the position shown in Fig. 96*a* the legs are swung from the hips, unjacking the body (Fig. 96*b*) and when they are checked in their movement angular momentum transfers to the whole body, which then turns into a sitting position on the table (Fig. 96*c*). (See also Appendix, demonstrations B and C.)

Transference can be sudden, as happens when a rotating body part is checked abruptly, or it can be gradual, as the arm, leg, etc., only gradually loses its angular speed. The phenomenon is common to dancing and athletic movement where, often, angular momentum is

---

* To determine (b) (i.e. the angular momentum of his Centre of Gravity about the point of take-off) the formula MVR is more convenient: where the jumper's mass (M) moves with a velocity (V) at a perpendicular distance to the point of take-off (R). Once the athlete leaves the board, V and R are changing constantly, under the force of gravity.

† 'English' to North Americans.

Figure 97

first developed and stored 'locally' while in contact with the ground and used, later, to turn the whole body in the air. The following are examples:

(i) Fig. 97. In a *tour en l'air*, the ballet dancer first rotates the arms, shoulders and head in a horizontal plane, with the feet firmly fixed on the floor. Then, as the legs drive him into the air, the effect transfers and his whole body twists.

(ii) A high-jumper's pronounced free leg swing at take-off can build up much of the angular momentum he will need subsequently for the lay-out over the crossbar (Fig. 140*k–w*).

(iii) On the springboard the diver develops angular momentum by swinging his arms (Fig. 98*a*, *b*). This helps to turn his body in the air (Fig. 98*c*).

'Local' angular momentum is best built up with the body part extended and accelerating through a considerable arc and about an axis

Figure 98

a   b   c

95

coincident in direction with that of the turning effect required after transfer; for angular momentum, being a vector quantity, has direction as well as magnitude.* Maximum angular velocity should be developed before contact with the ground is broken. On transference, the effect on the whole body depends on the distance of the axis of 'localised' movement from the body's main axis, as well as the magnitude and direction of the 'local' angular momentum. In Fig 98, for example, the turning effect of the arms on the body is all the more powerful because of the distance between the shoulder line and the body's main axis passing through the diver's Centre of Gravity. For, in effect, it is the arms' angular momentum about the main axis which is important. (See also page 109.)

Figure 99

Eccentric thrust. As, on successive take-offs, an athlete's line of thrust moves progressively farther, perpendicularly, from his Centre of Gravity, so will body rotation be easier and the projection of his Centre of Gravity be more difficult. (See *Moments*, page 69.) Thus, angular momentum can also be acquired by driving 'off centre', i.e. eccentrically.

In track and field athletics this type of thrust is usually applied to an athlete at a point where one foot is in contact with the ground—when its line of action is often at a considerable perpendicular distance to his Centre of Gravity. However, the transmitting of a *large* force from the ground to the athlete can take place only when the thrust passes close to his hip, knee and ankle joint and to his Centre of Gravity (Fig. 99) Otherwise there is a tendency for these joints to collapse and the thrust develops angular momentum beyond the athlete's ability to control it. (See also *Impulse*, page 36.)

The following are examples of eccentric thrust:

* Foucault's experiment of 1851 (repeated dramatically at the entrance to the U.N. Building, New York), exemplifies the directional quality of angular momentum. A heavy ball, suspended approximately 200 ft, is set swinging to and fro over several hours. A large compass dial beneath *appears* to record a continual change of swing in a clockwise direction—due to the fact that, in the Northern Hemisphere, *the earth is rotating counter-clockwise.* In fact, the pendulum retains its plane of motion, regardless of the earth's rotation.

(i) By bringing his head and arms forward, as a preliminary to his downward thrust against the springboard, the diver moves his Centre of Gravity slightly forward of his feet (Fig. 58*b*, *c*). In a good dive the required turning effect is combined with sufficient height off the board (see pages 69–71).

(ii) Although not perceptible in good jumping, part of a high-jumper's lay-out over the crossbar is due to an eccentric leg thrust at take-off (Fig. 90). But the best jumpers sacrifice only a fraction of their upward spring to obtain sufficient rotation (Fig. 91). They gain more from their position at the high point than they lose in take-off velocity.

(iii) In a gainer (i.e. reverse) dive (Fig. 100) angular momentum is imparted to the body by means of a final foot thrust, often made with the toes gripping the end of the springboard. This is all the more effective because of its distance from the diver's Centre of Gravity.

(iv) In initiating a front somersault, with no travel, on a trampoline the performer 'breaks' at the hips (Fig. 101). The reaction of the trampoline thus projects him vertically, with a forward somersault. (Here, the total horizontal momentum generated while the feet are in contact with the trampoline must be zero. This means that if, at this time, he imparts momentum backward to some part of his body, e.g., in rotating the arms clockwise, he must give the rest of his body equal momentum forward, e.g., by shifting his hips horizontally in an opposite direction. Thus the trampoline will have exerted no residual force horizontally.)

Figure 100

Figure 101

(*The checking of linear momentum is, in fact, caused by an eccentric thrust, whereas a transference of angular momentum produces such a thrust.*)

Turns originating in the air

Action and reaction. While Newton's Third Law applies to all motion, it is particularly important to an understanding of human and animal movement which begins in the air, 'free' in space. For whereas take-off surfaces can 'absorb' the reactions to turns originated on the ground, the body alone can do this when initiating movement in the air. (See also Appendix, demonstration D.)

By way of comparison and illustration, we will consider two phases of a pike dive (Fig. 102). When the diver drives down on the springboard it reacts with equal force by thrusting upward against his feet; when, as a result, his body is thrown into the air, its linear and angular momenta are equal but opposite to that given to the earth; for impulse and angular impulse are common to both.

But later, when the diver 'pikes' in the air (Figs. 43 and 102), the muscles pulling the trunk down and forward, clockwise, act simultaneously on the thighs, pulling the legs upward in a counter-clockwise direction. Expressed in terms of the contraction of a single muscle, the fibres exert their force equally on origin and insertion, producing rotations on either side of the hip joint that are equal but opposite in their angular momenta. The muscle forces required to stop these rotations are also equal and opposite.

Here are some other examples of this phenomenon. If, from the position shown in Fig. 103a, the outstretched arm is swung horizontally across the body (Fig. 103b), the reaction moves the turntable and the standing athlete towards the arm; when the same action is executed after an upward jump (Fig. 104a, b) the body's reaction is even more pronounced (Fig. 104c). (This technique—with the arm lowered in front of the body and raised sideways again to repeat, if necessary— is sometimes used to create twist in dives, so 'squaring' the body for entry. But, in trampolining, such a method is too slow when attempting anything beyond a half-twist.)

As the long-jumper brings his legs forward and upward for the landing (Fig. 147) the hip flexor and abdominal muscles pull his upper body forward and downward. When the hurdler pulls the rear leg across the hurdle rail (Fig. 119a) the contracting muscles simultaneously twist the trunk towards the trailing leg. And when the discus thrower,

Figure 102

Figure 103

Figure 104

with both feet momentarily off the ground, twists his hips and legs in advance of his shoulders and the throwing arm (Fig. 187*d*), the acting muscles pull the upper parts of his body in an opposite direction.

With such movement, action and reaction occur in the same plane (e.g. Fig. 119*c*), or in planes that are parallel (e.g. Fig. 104*d* and Fig. 119*a*). They will be about an axis, an *axis of displacement*, always at right angles and passing through the athlete's Centre of Gravity (but not necessarily coinciding with his axis of momentum). Clockwise action produces counter-clockwise reaction, and vice versa, though it is possible that certain very minor reactions to movement can be taken up internally and, therefore, invisibly.

99

The importance of action-reaction in swimming is stressed by Counsilman.* 'It is important to realise that, although a swimmer may swim in an almost straight line, his movements to accomplish this are all circular or rotary, or variations and combinations of this type of movement. When the swimmer is in the water he is suspended in a fluid, and any circular movement of his arm, either in the recovery or the pull of his arm, or in the movement of his legs, will tend to have a reaction which will distort his body alignment in the opposite direction.' (Fig. 105).

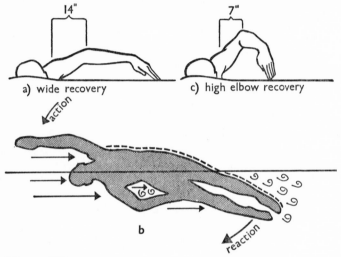

Figure 105

In the crawl, a poor arm recovery (due, usually, to insufficient shoulder flexibility) (Fig. 105a) can cause hips and legs to move in an opposite direction, increasing the swimmer's frontal and eddy resistance (Fig. 105b). This effect can be minimised by decreasing the arm's radius of rotation (Fig. 105c), i.e. by lifting the elbow and bringing the hand in. (After Figs. 1-4 and 1-13 of *The Science of Swimming*, James E. Counsilman, Prentice-Hall Inc., U.S.A.).

Relative moments of inertia. The angular velocity of the two moving body parts is inversely proportional to their moments of inertia about their common axis. Referring again to the pike dive (Figs. 43 and 102); assuming the moment of inertia of arms, head and trunk about the hips to be three times greater than that of the legs, the contracting muscles will impart angular velocities in the ratio of 1:3, i.e. while the trunk rotates through 30 deg. the legs describe a right angle.

* James E. Counsilman, *The Science of Swimming*, Prentice Hall Inc., Englewood Cliffs, N. J., U.S.A., 1st edition 1968, page 24.

Figure 106　　　　　　　　a　　　　　　　　b

If the man on the turntable adopts a sitting position (Fig. 106*a*) and then repeats the arm experiment, his rotation towards the extended arm (Fig. 106*b*) is reduced in comparison with the previous example (Fig. 103) because of his body's greater moment of inertia about a vertical axis. By the same token, a high-hurdler's body is less affected by the movements of his trailing leg when he leans forward (Fig. 133). On the other hand, a long-jumper preparing for landing will get his heels higher, through quicker and with the minimum of trunk reaction by first bringing the legs forward flexed (Fig. 150*d*) before extending them (Fig. 150*e*). It is therefore possible to control the angular range and speed of reaction to some extent.

We have seen that movement originated in the air cannot disturb an athlete's Centre of Gravity; thus, in piking (Figs. 43 and 102), when the upper body and arms and lower legs are brought forward in relation to the Centre of Gravity, the hips, lower trunk and upper parts of the thighs move back, and the product of the masses and their distances about the Centre of Gravity is unchanged.

Control of reaction-location. Within certain limits an athlete can control the location of body reaction. We have seen how the turntable reacts to an arm movement in a horizontal plane; but when both arms are swung in opposite directions simultaneously (Fig. 107*a*, *b*), the reaction to the movement of

Figure 107

Figure 108

one arm is 'absorbed' by the other and the turntable does not move. A similar action of the arms after an upward jump (Fig. 108) will not affect the body. Again, a high-jumper's clockwise arm sweep (Fig. 109a, b) could produce a counter-clockwise reaction of the body, or it could be 'absorbed' by the other arm (Fig. 109c) or some other part.

Figure 109

When a hurdling rear leg movement is performed on a turntable, the reaction swings the table in an opposite direction (Fig. 110a and b); but if the arms are used correctly, they can absorb this reaction and the table remains still (c). In hurdling, this arm action keeps the trunk facing the front to the advantage of balance, direction and speed on landing.

Again, in swimming the crawl stroke with a wide, flat arm recovery (Fig. 111) the alignment of the hips (which, otherwise, would swing laterally in reaction) can be cancelled out by a two-beat cross-over kick.

Illusions. While, doubtless, a working knowledge of the mechanics of movement improves what has been called 'the coaching eye', action and reaction in the air are often difficult for even an experienced

a   b   c

Figure 110

person to detect because of rotation or spin developed at take-off. To explain: when a pike dive is well executed (Fig. 102) it appears that throughout the upward part of the flight the diver brings his upper body down towards fixed legs and then, keeping the arms, head and trunk still, throws the legs back on a fixed trunk to assume a straight position for entry (Fig. 102). Trunk and leg motions seem isolated and without reaction.

This is because the diver leaves the springboard with forward rotation. In piking, as we have seen, the legs are in fact pulled towards the trunk but, in a good dive, their angular velocity is approximately equal to the body's rotational speed in an opposite direction; thus the legs remain almost vertical as the trunk rotates down and forward.

Conversely, the trunk movement is the more pronounced during the upward flight because it blends with the body's overall forward rotation off the board. Later, in straightening out, the trunk rotates backward and the legs forward in an approximate ratio of 1:3, but the body's take-off rotation cancels out the trunk movement while greatly speeding up the movement of the legs (Fig. 102). *Thus, the diver's total angular momentum is first concentrated in the trunk and then in the legs.*

The following are examples from track and field athletics. The pole vaulter's eccentric arm thrust at the top of the vault (Fig. 112*a*) imparts a rotation (clockwise in our illustration) to his whole body. But as he simultaneously 'arches' or 'jacks', pulling the trunk and legs in towards each other, the leg movement is the more apparent to an onlooker because it blends with the vaulter's overall clockwise rotation. But

103

As the left arm recovers from position (a), the right leg is kicked horizontally (b) to absorb the reaction and then thrusts downward (c). Now the left leg has crossed over the right and is ready to kick sideways (e) as the right arm recovers (d). (After Fig. 11-8 of *The Science of Swimming*, James E. Counsilman, Prentice-Hall, Inc., U.S.A., page 32.)

Rear view

Figure 111

when, on releasing the pole, he 'unjacks' his body (Fig. 112) overall rotation favours the lifting of the arms, head and chest, and the counterclockwise leg reaction is hardly noticeable, or, perhaps, is completely nullified.

Similarly, the muscles pulling the hurdler's leading leg towards the ground also straighten up his trunk; at this stage of clearance he, too, 'unjacks' (Fig. 119c). But because of taking off with an overall forward rotation his trunk maintains a forward lean for the landing and the

Figure 112   a   b

leading leg sweeps down and back even more quickly. Likewise, in long-and high-jumping, action and reaction in the air are sometimes difficult to discern and analyse through being 'superimposed' upon rotations of the whole body.

We have seen already (page 85) that an arm or leg can be moving

Figure 113

relative to other parts of the body without force acting simultaneously. Theoretically, therefore, force can be applied to a limb while an athlete is in contact with the ground and, relative to the trunk, the limb will go on moving in the air without apparent reaction, for the reaction will have taken place on the ground. However, usually with body movement, where there is motion there is force also, because of the internal resistances which must be overcome.

Exploitation of relative moments of inertia. We know that movement originating in the air cannot change an athlete's total angular momentum about his axis of momentum (see page 86) because the action of one part of his body is 'cancelled out' by the reaction of another. Hence, it might appear that it is impossible to turn the whole body in the air without a *point d'appui*. However, the following examples will prove to the contrary:

(i) If a man, freely falling through space or standing on a frictionless turntable, extends his arms (Fig. 113a) and then swings them horizontally in, say, a clockwise direction, the lower parts of his body will then turn in a counter-clockwise direction (Fig. 113b). And when he lowers his arms and takes the twist out of his abdominal muscles by turning his shoulders counter-clockwise, a clockwise reaction is produced in his hips and legs. However, now that the moment of inertia of the shoulders and arms is so much smaller than when the arms were extended, the clockwise reaction of his lower body is slight. In consequence, the whole of his body has turned counter-clockwise (Fig. 113c).

(ii) This process—sometimes used at the completion of the twist, in a twisting somersault dive, to bring the hips and legs into line with the upper body—is similar to that which enables a cat or rabbit, dropped from an upside-down position, to twist in the air and land on its feet (Fig. 114). During the first stage of its fall the animal 'pikes' or bends in the middle and stretches out its hind legs almost pependicular to an axis passing through its trunk (Fig. 114*b*). It then twists the fore part of its body through 180 deg.; the head, fore legs and upper trunk are now ready for the landing. The hind parts react by being displaced through a much smaller angle, because of their much greater moment of inertia about this axis (Fig 114*c*).

During the second stage of the animal's fall twisting takes place about a new axis approximately parallel with its hind legs (Fig. 114*c*), the twist being in the same direction as that of the head and trunk during the first phase. Therefore the hind legs now turn through the larger angle, for the moment of inertia of its upper body about this new axis is much greater (Fig. 114*d*). At the completion of this series of movements the animal's whole body is free from deformation and has turned through 180 deg. (Fig. 114). In our illustration the rabbit turns about these two axes of displacement at different times. However, the movements can be—and often are—made *simultaneously*.

Likewise, when a diver assumes

Figure 114

a b c d

e f g h

i j k l

(From *Manual of Diving*,
Amateur Swimming Asso-
ciation, England)

Figure 115

a front-arch position, 'breaking' at the hips (Fig. 115), extended legs and
hips can be used to rotate the trunk in an opposite direction. But to
originate twists in the air by this method (and 540-deg. twists have been
claimed for divers using a one metre board) the body must be neither
too straight nor too 'piked'; and considerable spinal flexibility is required to continue the movement forward, laterally and backward.

(iii) An outstanding example of the use of this principle in sport is
seen in the half-twisting somersault, piked, dive (Fig. 116). The diver
leaves the board with forward rotation (Fig. 116*a*) and then adopts a

107

Figure 116

pike position (Fig. 116*b*). Now he twists his trunk through 90 deg. and *then* extends his arms sideways (Fig. 116*c*).

With the moment of inertia of the head, arms and trunk now greatly increased about the body's long axis, the legs are momentarily brought into line and twist taken out of the abdominal muscles (Fig. 116*c, d*); their twist continues until a pike position has again been assumed, but with the legs now on the side of the trunk farthest from take-off (Fig. 116*d*).

These leg movements produce no noticeable reaction or change of position in the rest of the diver's body because of (*a*) the latter's greater moment of inertia about the trunk's long axis, and (*b*) the illusion created by his forward rotation off the springboard—a rotation in the sagittal plane which tends to conceal his upper body's reaction to leg movement in that plane.

The diver has again assumed a pike position, but with his body still twisted (Fig. 116*d*). He then brings his arms back to their first position, stretched above his head, afterwards completing a 90-deg. trunk turn (Fig. 116*e*). Finally, now facing the springboard, he straightens out and enters the water (Fig. 116).

Just as animals employ these movements without conscious analysis of the mechanics involved so, too, can athletes. And just as animals do not all conform precisely to the same movement pattern when faced with such problems of balance and safety so, too, in diving and other forms of athletic technique do methods of exploitation vary from one person to another. In originating twisting movement in the air, for example, there are many variations of head, shoulder, trunk, arm, hip and leg movement available to the flexible, physically-clever performer. (Diving experiments appear to demonstrate that about three-quarters of twisting originating in the air is developed through the use of the spine; only about a quarter through hip movement.)

To re-emphasise: these movements of the whole body in space always take place about axes of displacement which pass through the body's Centre of Gravity, but which, in most cases, are distinct from its axes of rotation and momentum (see also page 100). They cannot change total angular momentum.

Secondary axes. Another type of movement involving the exploitation of relative moments of inertia is concerned with motion of a part of an athlete about an axis at a distance from his Centre of Gravity—a 'local' or 'secondary' axis.

From Newton's Third Law it follows that when a man falling freely through space, or standing on a frictionless turntable, twirls an arm in a circle above his head so that its axis of movement corresponds with the body's longitudinal axis, the angular momentum thus devel-

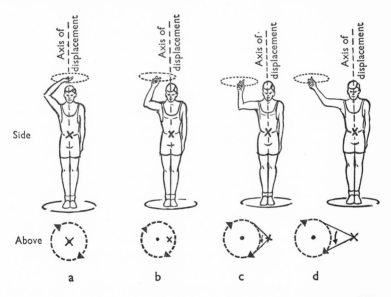

Figure 117

oped is simultaneously compensated for by turning *the whole body mass in an opposite direction* In such a circumstance the arm action possesses a constant turning effect on the rest of the body (Fig. 117*a*).

(*Note*. The arm's radius of gyration shown in Fig. 117 is the horizontal distance between its axis and a point which represents the sum of all the separate moments of inertia of its many parts; a point where, *for the purpose of rotation only*, we can consider the mass of the arm to be concentrated. It is *not* the arm's Centre of Gravity. The circle traced out by this radius will be referred to as the *circle of gyration*, see Fig. 82.)

When a similar movement is made slightly to the side, however, the turning effect is in proportion to the arm's distance from the axis of displacement (Fig. 117*b*). In reaction, greatest angular displacement is produced when the arm is farthest from this main axis, and least when nearest, but the total rotational effect on the whole body (as a result of a 360-deg. arm movement) is the same as before.

Should the axis of arm action (now a *secondary axis*) be moved so far to the side that the arm's circle of gyration no longer 'embraces' the axis of displacement (Fig. 117*c*), then part of the arm movement produces a turning effect on the rest of the body *contrary* to that hitherto; for, relative to the axis of displacement, the arm moves through a sector of the circle of gyration in an opposite direction. However, when the arm is farthest from the body's main axis its turning effect exceeds that of our two previous examples and, through a 360-deg. arm movement, the angular displacement of the whole body remains the same.

Fig. 117*d* shows how, with a further increase in distance between these two axes, the sector producing a contrary rotation is enlarged. By virtue of the greater distance between these axes it is also more powerful, but so, too, is the arm's turning effect in an opposite direction. Therefore, through 360 deg. of arm movement, the angular displacement of the whole body is the same as before.

It should be noted that the secondary axis of each rotating arm in Figs. 103, 104, 106, 107, 108 and 109 passes through the shoulder, the main axis passing through the man's Centre of Gravity. For the purpose of illustrating a principle, Fig. 117 has been over-simplified; for the movements of the arm are not shown to have an effect on the lateral displacement of the rest of the body, relative to its Centre of Gravity, as would be the case with a man falling freely through space.

Here it should be stressed that

(i) while the arm movement continues the body can be turned horizontally through any required angle; but when the arm stops, the body stops also;

(ii) although the foregoing examples show motion in a horizontal plane, the phenomenon applies to motion in any plane;

(iii) such movement cannot change the body's total angular momentum about its axis of momentum.

In effect, therefore, it is the arm's angular momentum about the body's main axis (passing through the Centre of Gravity) which is significant.

Balance in the air. Movements which exploit relative moments of inertia are of particular importance to the maintenance of an athlete's balance in the air, for they can be used to counteract embarrassing rotations either originated at take-off or caused by air and wind resistance after contact with the ground has been broken. The following turntable experiment exemplifies this.

If angular momentum in *the same clockwise or counter-clockwise direction* is given to the man and turntable *before* he makes any of the arm movements described under *Secondary axes* (Fig. 117), the reaction to them will create an illusion of reducing total angular momentum or even of reversing its direction, depending upon the efficiency of the arm movements; but when the arm stops, the original angular momentum is again apparent. (See also Appendix demonstration E.)

Three examples taken from sport follow:

(i) A ski jumper with forward rotation in the air (movement hardly conducive to a safe landing!) can move his arms about his shoulders,

a   b

Figure 118

in the same vertical plane and in the same direction as the embarrassing body rotation, and thus take up some of it, causing his body rotation to slow down. However, when the arm movement stops, the original body rotation again reveals itself (Fig. 118*a*).

Factors limiting the value of this action to the ski jumper are (*a*) working together in a sagittal plane, the arms cannot be swung with full range behind the shoulders and (*b*) as they move past the trunk they could possibly *add* to the body's forward rotation (for the reason given under *Secondary axes*).

(ii) In the hitch-kick long-jumping technique (Fig. 147) the forward rotation of the arms and the movement of the legs have a forward angular momentum. This may be (*a*) less than, (*b*) equal to, or (*c*) greater than the forward angular momentum with which the jumper left the board, depending upon the take-off angular momentum and the efficiency of his arm and leg movements in the air.

In the first case (*a*) the arms and legs will take up some of his angular momentum, causing his forward rotation to slow down. In (*b*) they will take up all his angular momentum, and so his forward rotation will cease temporarily; and in (*c*) the trunk will automatically rotate backward about the body's Centre of Gravity, otherwise the jumper will have generated angular momentum in the air, which is impossible.

(iii) The long-jumper corrects lateral balance (i.e. his movement in a frontal plane) by the use of his arms (Fig. 118*b*). When they are moved about his head in that plane their influence on the rotation of his whole body is the more powerful because of the distance between his shoulders (secondary axes) and his Centre of Gravity (through which must pass his axis of displacement). Depending upon its efficiency, the arm action slows down, stops or even reverses body rotation, yet without changing his total angular momentum; when the arms stop, the rotation of his whole body 'takes over' again.

It is sometimes convenient to 'break down' movement originating in the air into simultaneous rotation in several planes. Thus, a combination of rear leg recovery and front leg downward drive in hurdling may be considered as simultaneous body rotations and reactions in the three main planes, i.e. transverse, frontal and sagittal (Figs. 119*a*, *b* and *c*).

We have already seen (page 102) that, in a transverse plane, the action of the hurdler's lower limbs twists his upper body towards the trailing leg (Fig. 119*a*); in a frontal plane it also tilts it down in the direction of

112

Figure 119

this leg (Fig. 119*b*); and in a sagittal plane the reaction rotates him backward, as in a hitch-kick (Fig. 119*c*). In all three planes, clockwise motion produces simultaneous counter-clockwise reaction, and vice versa; in each case angular momenta are equal but opposite.

These principles of balance and reaction also apply to certain kinds of movement when an athlete is in contact with the ground. If a man balancing on a beam feels he is falling to one side, he might regain balance by rotating his extended arms *in the same direction,* as with the maintenance of lateral balance of the long-jumper in the air (Fig. 118*b*), with the difference, however, that when in contact with a beam the movement could, at the same time, displace his Centre of Gravity. In running, too, the alignment of the body (both on and off the ground) depends to some extent upon such principles.

Balance in motion in all sport is, to greater or lesser degree, influenced by the factors discussed both here and under *Forces* (2): *Balance in motion* on page 61 and *friction* on page 58.

Nutation and gyration

So far, we have generally assumed the total angular momentum of a rotating athlete (in contact with the ground or free in space) to be expressed in such a manner that the theoretical axis of momentum and his overt axis of rotation coincide, are unchanging in their relationship and are therefore fixed in direction. In Fig. 120*a* the body's longitudinal axis and in *b* its medial axis are examples of such stable rotation—both being due to the imparting of an angular impulse about only *one* principal axis of the body. (For, in the posture shown, rotation about any other axis through the Centre of Gravity—*including the body's transverse axis*—will not possess this stability.)

Figure 120

Figure 121

a

Figure 122

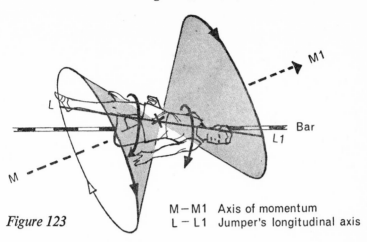

M — M1   Axis of momentum
L — L1   Jumper's longitudinal axis

Figure 123

The more marked the difference between the body's moments of inertia about its three principal axes, the easier it is to achieve conditions closely approximating to Fig. 120*a* and *b*; and, because the body's medial and transverse moments of inertia are so nearly equal, *b* could almost be regarded as rotation about *any* axis through the Centre of Gravity at right angles to the longitudinal axis. (Note: In the posture shown it happens that *a* and *b* show body-axes of minimum and maximum moments of inertia respectively. But with the athlete in a different position (piked, for example, Fig. 121) the transverse axis might be the one associated with maximum moment of inertia and it would be difficult to determine a longitudinal axis.)

Such movement as has been described above is, in fact, a rare phenomenon in athletics, for it is extremely difficult to impart rotation about only one principal axis—usually *some* rotation is developed about one or both of the other two principal axes, albeit inadvertently; in order to perform properly, an athlete has usually to develop angular momentum about his transverse axis or about more than one of his principal axes simultaneously. Under such a circumstance his motion can often be described in terms of *twisting about his longitudinal axis, together with a simultaneous "gyrating" of this axis about the axis of momentum*—i.e. with these axes no longer coinciding.

Thus, the axis of momentum of a high jumper leaving the ground with twist about his longitudinal axis while rotating forward about his transverse axis (Fig. 122*a*) (with their associated angular momenta,

115

Figure 124

shown in Fig. 122*b* in the ratio of 1:2) will be fixed in direction at the angle illustrated, with its diagrammatic length appropriately proportioned. In the air the jumper will twist about his longitudinal axis

116

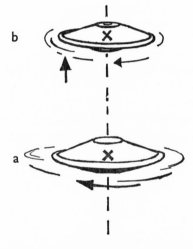

Figure 125

which, at the same time, will commence to describe* a closed conical path about his axis of momentum, so that if he originates no movement in the air, *this conical path will not vary and there will be no interchange of angular momentum between these two rotational motions* (Fig. 123).

With different initial angular impulses about the principal axes (causing, therefore, different proportions of angular momenta) the closed path described will be changed in size. When that path is very small indeed (apparent only as a nodding or wobbling of the longitudinal axis as it moves around the axis of momentum) it is usually referred to as *nutation;* whereas a marked conical motion, too great to be regarded as mere nutation, may more conveniently be called *gyration.*

* In high jumping, a *complete* conical path is never traced out.

The trading of angular momentum

Although, as we have seen (page 86), a freely-rotating athlete cannot change his total angular momentum and, under the conditions described above, will experience no interchange of angular momenta between gyration and twisting, *through action and reaction he can redispose body-mass, relative to his axis of momentum, and so alter the direction of his principal axes* to (a) rid himself of the complexities of multi-axial rotation by stabilizing his rotation about only one of them, or conversely (b) deliberately bring about gyration.

Thus, a gymnast somersaulting forward as he leaves the trampoline (i.e. rotating forward about a transverse axis) (Fig. 124a) can originate movement in the air (Fig.124b–e) which causes a change of direction of his body's principal axes. In consequence, he absorbs some angular momentum by twisting about his longitudinal axis, simultaneously changing the initial somersaulting about the transverse axis into the motion illustrated (Fig. 124f–i). In this case, the size of the cone-angle described by the longitudinal axis will be fairly large, because his moment of inertia about this axis is comparatively small.

The initiation of a twisting about the longitudinal axis does not alter the *rate* at which the somersaulting takes place—providing there is no change in the body's moment of inertia about transverse and medial axes; the angular velocity of gyration about the axis of momentum remains the same.* But, of course, if the twisting is rapid and the cone-angle therefore very much reduced, the motion will not *look* so much like a somersault. Likewise, by originating movement in the air (i.e. through action and reaction) a straddle high jumper, for example, can bring his longitudinal axis more into line with his axis of momentum and so twist more rapidly away from the bar—more effective than the mere reduction of his moment of inertia about his longitudinal axis (as discussed on page 87).

However, in Fig. 124, where, in the process of displacing his principal axes, the gymnast has *increased* his moment of inertia about his medial and transverse axes (changing from a piked to an extended position:

---

* For the plane of the body's rotation in the somersault before the twist starts (i.e. the plane at right angles to the axis of momentum) changes slightly as the twist is originated, reducing the body's moment of inertia about this axis. (Compare Fig. 124a with f.)

With the same angular velocity about the axis of momentum but a smaller moment of inertia, the angular momentum due to the somersault is less than it was—the rest appearing in the form of a twist.

compare *a* with *f–j*), the angular velocity of gyration *decreases*, as it does whenever the moment of inertia is increased.

In general, trampolinists, divers, etc., initiate their twists from somersaults, so that considerable angular momentum about the transverse axis is then available for 'trading' around the longitudinal axis.

Precession

Whereas nutation and gyration involve no change in total angular momentum, *precession* does. Thus, a discus leaves the (right) hand with angular momentum primarily about its axis of greatest moment of inertia (Fig. 125*a*). (*Primarily*, because this axis will nutate about the axis of momentum.) When a lifting component of force acts to the left of this axis (as seen from the throwing position) the force has a clockwise turning effect on the discus, imparting a new angular momentum to it in the same clockwise sense (Fig. 125*b*).

As a consequence of this constantly-applied turning effect, the axis of momentum changes direction (an effect called *precession*) and the discus automatically corrects its attitude to conform, tilting its forward edge upwards (Fig. 125*c*; see also page 204, *The flight of the discus*). Although eccentrically-applied forces (and, therefore, precessional movement) are in operation in all athletic techniques, only in discus throwing are they sometimes apparent and of any real consequence.

PART II : CHAPTER SIX

Running

Running, 'the classical athletic sport',* can be considered both simple and difficult: simple, because it is an instinctive, natural skill performed at some time by all but the most unfortunate; difficult in its mechanical complexity.

No two athletes run in precisely the same way, for people vary in their anatomic structure and body proportion, in strength and flexibility, in posture (often influenced by characteristics of personality) and in their interpretation of some fundamental phase of running action. Moreover, the emphasis on particular aspects of form changes from one running event to another. The ancient Greeks were aware of this; Philostratus of Lemnos speaks of sprinters 'moving their legs with their arms to achieve speed, as if winged by their hands'; and Aristotle analyses aspects of running in his *On the Gait of Animals*.

Yet all the many kinds of running, from the shortest sprint to races over the longest distances, share certain basic mechanical principles, a knowledge of which is helpful not only to an understanding of running itself, but in the analysis of other track and field events and sports. For many skills are derived from or are influenced by these innate running movements.

Running movement is brought about by a combination of forces: *internally*, muscular force, producing a change in ground reaction, as well as overcoming resistance due to muscle viscosity, the tensions of fascia, ligaments, tendons, etc.; *externally*, the force of gravity, the resistance of the air and the forces exerted by the ground on the runner's shoe (to ensure that the ground can exert a maximum forward force, the runner wears spiked shoes; see also page 58).

Compared with the locomotion of modern machines, human locomotion is cumbersome and inefficient, for it depends upon the rotation of legs and arms, i.e. approximately 47 per cent of the body's total mass,

* J. Lindhard, *Theory of Gymnastics* (Methuen & Co. Ltd, England, 2nd edition 1939), page 321.

120

Running

and their moments of inertia necessitate the use of tremendous muscular force and expenditure of energy to start, retard, stop or reverse limb movement. In terms of effort economy a wheel mechanism is far better; but Nature uses only rods and levers, arms and legs.

The human body is designed for accuracy of control rather than mere mechanical efficiency, however, and its combined adaptiveness, elasticity and strength have never been equalled by machines. In particular, the three leg levers, articulated on the pelvis, adapt themselves admirably to an enormous variety of postures, efforts and movements, of which running is only one.

Good running calls for a co-ordinated action of the entire body. However, for the purpose of movement analysis it is convenient to consider it in various parts and phases.

Leg action

Running speed is the product of *length* and *frequency* of stride, their ratio changing from one phase of a race to another and from athlete to athlete. Yet these two factors are always interdependent, and maximum running efficiency exists only when they are in correct proportion, depending, mainly on the weight, build, strength, flexibility and co-ordination of the runner.

Fig. 126 represents the complete cycle of leg movement, i.e. over two strides. It divides naturally into phases of *recovery*, when the leg swings from the hip with its foot clear of the ground, and *drive*, when the foot is in contact with the ground. Both are finely co-ordinated.

Recovery phase. The instant the toes leave the ground the foot, which had been brought momentarily to rest, undergoes an acceleration, when the leg flexes at the hip, knee and ankle joints (Fig. 126a to e). This appears to be the result of (i) a reflex mechanism which prevents over-extension and (ii) the forward motion of the thigh causing (iii) a transference of angular momentum to the foreleg. These flexions are marked, particularly, in sprinting.

In this way the mass of the leg is brought closer to the hip axis, reducing the leg's moment of inertia and increasing angular velocity. The work of pulling the leg mass forward and upward (mainly that of the hip flexors, supported by the abdominals) is also reduced because of the tapering of leg mass; for the arrangement of the muscles ensures that the comparatively light calf and foot, distant from the hip, are easier to accelerate (a principle which also applies to the arms).

The co-ordination of both legs is so timed that the flexion of the

121

Figure 126 a b c d e

recovery leg is greatest, and its back-kick highest, fractionally after the front foot meets the ground (Fig. 126*d*). The swinging thigh then begins forward-upward movement of great importance to the runner's drive; the acceleration of this thigh increases the force exerted by the ground, thus increasing the speed with which the Centre of Gravity is moved away from the supporting foot.

At the limit of its forward swing (coinciding with the completion of rear leg drive, Fig. 126*f*) thigh movement is reversed, the leg extends from the knee joint and the foot accelerates first forward and then backward (Fig. 126*g* and *h*). The reversal of thigh movement (brought about primarily by the glutei and hamstring muscles) produces a transference of angular momentum and flail-like action in the fore leg; yet the movement is smooth and neuromuscularly controlled.

It is important to note that in efficient running the leading foot is never stretched grotesquely for a longer stride; *stride length is the product of a driving forward of the entire body.*

The recovery phase is much more the result of muscular control than a pendulum action. It takes longer than the driving phase and for about half the time on each stride, when both feet are off the ground, the legs recover simultaneously. This is in contrast to a walking action, in which the legs swing for not more than half the stride duration, never more than one at a time and contact with the ground is unbroken (Fig. 127).

Driving phase. The foot lands:

(i) First, on the outside edge, and with the toes pointing slightly outward. It then takes the full weight of the body at a point which varies with the runner's speed; in sprinting, well up on the ball of the foot, almost flat-footed at very low speeds. As the body passes

122

f   g   h   i   j   k

over the foot, the heel touches the ground lightly. These movements
are an instinctive, *natural* phenomenon.

(ii) With its leg flexed at the knee joint, 'giving' on impact (Fig.
126*c*, *d*); knee and ankle axes are parallel.

(iii) Ideally, with a backward speed, relative to the runner's Centre
of Gravity, at least equal to his forward speed over the ground (see
page 58).

(iv) In front of the Centre of Gravity; the distance diminishes with
an increase in speed.

The optimum position of the feet in running is one in which their
inner borders fall approximately along a single straight line. When one
foot is placed directly in front of the other, lateral balance is impaired.
Too wide a spacing (sometimes due to large thighs or knock knees)
encourages a 'weaving' running action.

Experts are not agreed on whether the leg's backward movement can
be used to 'pull' the runner over the foot before the 'push' of the
drive. Some say it is impossible, while others rate it purely incidental
to grounding the foot quickly for another drive. Still others recommend
a deliberate pulling action.

Mechanically, pulling and pushing forces are equally efficient: e.g.
it is all the same whether a railway engine pushes or pulls; but with
the human machine pushing forces are much stronger. The formation
of the leg is unsuited to a pulling force, for the resultant of the ground's
reaction to such a force and the upthrust of the ground on the foot
cannot pass through the runner's Centre of Gravity (see Fig. 131*a*, which
shows a sprinter's eighth stride from the blocks). Hence, to attempt to
accelerate the Centre of Gravity by this means is a waste of effort (page
70). Distance runners (who, in conserving a little energy on each stride,

123

a   b   c   d   e   f

Figure 127

The Walking Action (a–f). Walking differs from running in that (1) contact with the ground is unbroken and, momentarily, both feet touch the ground simultaneously on each stride—in a period of "double-support". As a result (2) the supporting-driving phase of leg movement takes longer than the recovery phase, the legs swinging one at a time. Also (3) the body attains its greatest height as it passes over the supporting leg (*c*) and is lowest with the legs widespread (*a, f*); the hip action peculiar to race walking is used to eliminate this rise and fall on each stride. As the walking pace is increased (*d, e, f*), the period of double-support shortens, the strides lengthen and quicken and the hips assume a lower position as the front foot meets the ground (*f*). With an increase in walking speed, the legs swing with increased angular velocity, so that the time taken in recovery is almost constant. Force patterns* (as recorded on force platforms) almost invariably indicate the favouring of one leg over the other; and these are affected by walking speed, body build and age.

save a great deal over the full distance) should therefore reject the 'pulling' theory on grounds of effort economy.

As for sprinters, they can obtain and benefit from this second impulse *provided* the front foot has backward motion, relative to the ground, as touchdown occurs. Obviously, such a method of acceleration becomes progressively more difficult as the athlete gathers forward speed; and at top speed there can be little—if any—relative motion as this foot contacts the track. (See page 58.) However, whereas the distance runner permits the lower leg to swing naturally as it approaches the ground, the sprinter's need for a rapid striding cadence (in good sprinting of about four and a half to five strides per second—it quickens *very* slightly with a progressive reduction in the stride-impulse) demands an emphasis on getting the front leg quickly under the body for a more immediate leg drive.

* A. H. Ismail, J. W. Banang and K. R. Manning, *Assessment and Evaluation o Hemiplegic Gait.* Purdue University and Crossroads Rehabilitation Centre, U.S.A., August 1965.

124

As the body moves over the foot (Fig. 126*i*, *j*) the thigh's backward motion (relative to the hips) is momentarily retarded, while flexion increases at the knee and ankle and the heel drops to touch the ground lightly. This gives the foot more time in which to apply force against the ground and stretches the extensor leg muscles. The lowering of body weight also reduces the athlete's moment of inertia about the supporting foot, making it easier and quicker to pivot over and beyond.

The supporting leg's accelerating effect on the runner increases progressively as he moves forward, and the leg is able to direct more of its driving force towards the body. However, the *forward force* reaches a maximum and then tapers off before contact with the ground is broken (Fig. 131). In good running, the *vertical component* of this force (approximately two and a half times body weight in sprinting) is never more than necessary to counteract the pull of gravity on each stride; but it usually exceeds the horizontal component—even in acceleration.

The gluteus maximus, hamstring, quadricep, gastrocnemius and hallucis longus muscles bear the burden of the movement. Extension originates in the stronger but slower muscles surrounding the runner's Centre of Gravity, and is taken up at the knee, ankle and foot, in that order. All extensions end together with the foot well behind the body (Fig. 126*k*)—again pointing slightly outward, with the runner breaking contact with the *inside* front edge.

Eccentric movement. In a normal standing position, a man's Centre of Gravity is situated approximately at the level of the upper third of the sacrum and, with the raising of various parts of the body, in running at times it is even higher. Fig. 128 illustrates how, relative to the athlete's Centre of Gravity, leg movement is eccentric, i.e. 'Off centre' (see pages 70 and 96).

Thus, while the force of reaction to the leg drive translates, or projects, the body's Centre of Gravity, its upward thrust tends to lift, and its forward thrust pushes forward, the corresponding hip (Fig. 128 which, for simplicity, shows the line of thrust actually passing through the

Figure 128

125

hips). Likewise, in recovery, the forward-upward swing encourages a retarding and dropping of the hip on the same side of the body. *In fact, hip action tends to reduce the thrust received from it or delivered to it.* The greater the effective leg drive, the more powerful these tendencies are; and as, in the course of the stride, the direction of the thrust or swing changes, so does the proportion of these horizontal and vertical reactions.

However, such hip movement is prevented by muscles and ligaments; e.g. as the body is first supported and then driven forward by one leg, the corresponding gluteus medius and minimus muscles prevent a sagging of the opposite hip. On the contrary, the hips *follow* the legs.

The reaction cannot be denied, however (see pages 28–30); *if the pelvis will not assimilate the by-product of eccentric leg thrust, then another part of the body, and/or the ground, must.*

Arm and shoulder action

Because of the muscular connections between the pelvis and the upper trunk (e.g. internal oblique and latissimus dorsi muscles) most of this reaction in running is absorbed by the upper body, which can be seen to twist rhythmically in opposition to the leg movement. However, a little is taken up internally and by the ground, and is therefore not apparent.

We have seen (page 101) that the location of body reaction can be controlled to some limited extent. In different types of running the reaction to the eccentric leg thrust is absorbed by:

(i) vigorous, but properly directed, arm action (as used in good sprinting; Fig. 129);

(ii) the shoulders and arms twisting *en bloc*, without a pivoting of the arms about the shoulders. This action was exemplified in the style of Emil Zatopek;

(iii) a combination of (i) and (ii) above, as is most common to all but the short sprinting events (Fig. 126).

Sprinting. In sprinting the accelerations of leg movement required for a striding cadence of four and a half to five times per second (the frequency in top-class competition) and for a powerful leg thrust, are possible only when the shoulders are kept steady about the trunk's longitudinal axis; because the trunk, with its great inertia, cannot twist and untwist with sufficient rapidity.

In good sprinting the reaction to the horizontal (i.e. twisting) component of the leg thrust is absorbed by the more easily controlled arms,

Figure 129 e   d   c   b   a

and the shoulders remain steady. However, to 'take up' this angular momentum, the arms have to operate with sufficient force and, primarily, in a sagittal (i.e. backward-forward) plane. Force of action is indicated by their radius and angular acceleration, while their range about the shoulders denotes the time/distance of force application. Arm action will tend to be more effective in absorbing 'twist' the greater its distance from the body's longitudinal axis.

Both forward and backward arm movements are part of a clockwise or counter-clockwise upper body twist; they work in sympathy with each other, not in opposition. During their forward swings they are kept flexed at about a right angle, giving great angular velocity and co-ordinating with the quick recovery action of the forward-swinging leg (Fig. 129*c, d, e*). *The forward arm movement* sets up a backward reaction on the corresponding shoulder, 'absorbing' the forward twisting which would otherwise ensue. Of particular importance here is the upper-arm movement in a sagittal plane; a slight cross-body swing of the lower arm is both natural and desirable.

The backward phase of arm action tends to thrust the corresponding shoulder forward. The arm's effect is at first strengthened and pro-longed by a natural straightening at the elbow, corresponding with the longer leverage of the driving leg on the opposite side. But towards the end of its backward movement the arm bends and speeds up again, to match the final, fast stages of leg drive (Fig. 129*e*).*

The range of arm movement in sprinting (as represented by the path of its Centre of Gravity) is about as much in front of as behind the shoulder axis. It varies with the individual (e.g. thin, small arms might

* The arms' varying length in swinging to and fro also prevents an undesirable turn of the body in a frontal plane—due to an eccentric leg thrust.

move through a greater arc) and, to a certain extent, from one phase of a sprint to another (emphasised, especially at the start); but usually, the hands swing no higher than shoulder level to the front, nor more than a foot behind the hip-line to the rear (Fig. 129).

While, in all forms of running, the primary function of the upper body is to 'take up' reaction to the eccentric leg drive, 'counter-balancing' and 'following' leg action, in sprinting particularly, the arms may be used to spur on the legs, which speed up and consequently add to their horizontal component of drive; for (as mentioned on page 28) action and reaction are interchangeable factors.

Since both arms accelerate upwards and downwards simultaneously (and, in sprinting, with values greater than gravitational acceleration) their subsequent downward retardation* and upward movement add to the vertical component of drive; and their downward acceleration, coinciding with touch down, lessens the impact between the ground and front foot—being most effective, in each case, when the arms are carried close to the trunk.

Moreover, by losing upward speed fractionally before the completion of leg drive, the arms ease the compression of the thrusting leg—and so permit more forceful and freer use of its foot and ankle. Hopper† writes: 'It is in this connection that the vital importance of timing becomes obvious; and one wonders how many pulled muscles and other troubles are due to temporary lack of exact co-ordination between leg and arm action.'

Longer distances. While wishing to maintain as high a speed as possible, those who run longer distances must conserve energy by reducing their effort and frequency of striding. Their weaker leg drive and slower leg swing in recovery develop less twisting angular momentum than in sprinting, and a reduced striding frequency gives the trunk time to take up the reaction to this angular momentum without re-course to forceful and tiring arm movement. Arm action is 'quieter' and does not fully compensate; hence the relaxed flowing shoulder-twist and gentle arm movement typical of the distance runner.

Trunk and head positions

Running movement can give maximum efficiency only when the athlete is properly balanced, which depends considerably upon the

---

* Which *constitutes an upward acceleration.*

† B. J. Hopper, 'Mechanics of Arm Action in Running' (*Track Technique*, U.S.A., No 17, September, 1964).

correct angling of the trunk. The following are relevant factors:
The force of the leg drive and the proportion of its horizontal and vertical components. As previously maintained (see pages 61, 66 and 67), for balanced running the moments of the vertical and horizontal components of drive must be adjusted about the runner's Centre of Gravity, and at uniform speed, can be considered constant: posture is almost erect though, when a good runner is viewed from the side, there is an illusion of a pronounced forward trunk lean when his driving leg is fully extended (Figs. 126*a* and 129*a*); a fairer view is obtained when he is in mid-stride (Figs. 126*d* and 129*d*).

However, in acceleration (i.e. in the gaining or losing of speed) the problem of balance is complicated because of variation in the horizontal component of leg drive. In positive acceleration, for example, the faster a man runs the more difficult it is for him to exert a large force against the ground which to him, seems to be receding rapidly; he is unable to move his feet fast enough. Thus, the force he exerts and its duration (i.e. the impulse) are successively reduced (see pages 36 and 37).

*(On leaving the blocks a sprinter will be in contact with the ground for approximately twice as long as when both feet are off the ground. After about ten strides the times will be equal; and, thereafter, will attain a ratio of between 1:1·3 and 1:1·5. At a maximum or near-maximum speed, while he is in contact with the ground in one unit of time he has to counteract the effect of gravity during 1·3 to 1·5 units— requiring an additional upward thrust of 1·3 to 1·5 times body weight. For his vertical component of drive must at all times keep him off the ground for sufficient time to get his legs into position for the next stride.)

For balance in varying accelerations a runner has constantly to alter the lever-arms of the force components by adjusting the position of his Centre of Gravity in relation to his supporting foot; this he achieves by changing the angle of his trunk (Fig. 130). In a phase of great positive acceleration (the result of a large horizontal component of force), as in the first stride from the blocks (Fig. 130*b* and *c*), a sprinter needs a pronounced forward lean; hence the main justification for a crouched start. But later in his race, with a reduction in the force he can exert, he has to assume a more erect position to avoid toppling forward (Fig. 130*f*). (*Note:* Here it is a vertical component of leg-drive *in excess*

---

* E. F. Housden. 'Mechanical analysis of the Running movement'. ('Run, Run, Run' by Fred Wilt *Track & Field News, Inc.*, U.S.A.)

Figure 130

of body weight on each stride which raises the sprinter's Centre of Gravity progressively towards a normal running position).

By the same token, balanced negative acceleration (as, for example, when sprinters slow down after breasting the tape) calls for a backward lean. An exaggerated lean either way reduces the stride length and places an unnecessary strain on the muscles of the trunk.

Rotation in a sagittal plane. So far, in considering the angling of the trunk, it has been convenient to assume the line of thrust from the ground reaction on each stride *always* to pass through a runner's Centre of Gravity. Certainly, the effect is as if it did so, and this approach to balance in running is recommended as most practical.

As Hopper* has shown, however, ground reaction, besides supporting and propelling the runner, may be considered to create angular momentum in a sagittal plane (Fig. 131), for when the foot first meets the track both vertical and horizontal components of reaction act in front of his Centre of Gravity, tending to rotate him *backwards* (Fig. 131*a*). Later, when a large vertical component acts behind his Centre of Gravity, the tendency is for the trunk to be rotated *forward* (Fig. 131*c–d*), and (particularly in acceleration), to be rotated *backward again* just before the foot breaks contact, when the vertical component has greatly diminished (Fig. 131*f*).

Hopper suggests that, to maintain the trunk in an efficient running position, the legs and arms 'take up' these angular momenta. Thus, with the line of thrust from the ground in front of the runner's Centre of Gravity, foreleg and forearm movements possess a counter clockwise angular momentum; and with this ground reaction behind, their effect is reversed. Finally, this 'absorbing' process is reversed yet again.

* B. J. Hopper. 'Rotation—a Vital Factor in Athletic Technique' (*Track Technique*, U.S.A., No. 10; December 1962 and March 1963: *Track & Field News*).

But Hopper says, '. . . the transmission of a big force from the ground to the body of the athlete will take place only when the line of its action passes close to both hip and the man's Centre of Gravity; so it is not surprising that the maximum ground reaction developed . . . in running does not occur until these conditions are fulfilled.'*

It seems likely that balance in running is dependent upon both methods, i.e. on the 'taking up' of embarrassing angular momenta, and the adjustment of the position of the Centre of Gravity to the force and direction of ground reaction.

Posture. Hip mobility is of special influence in determining the angle at which the trunk is held in running, because unusual flexibility in these joints enables an athlete to adjust his balance while maintaining a more upright position.

Other postural idiosyncracies can give an illusory, as opposed to real, trunk angle. Round shoulders and a tendency to stoop create an appearance of forward lean in running (Fig. 132*a*), while pigeon-chested or hollow-backed athletes appear to run with an upright carriage (Fig. 132*b*).

Posture, a product of heredity, environment and self-expression, is acceptable in an athlete if it permits the proper functioning of respiration, circulation, digestion, etc., and involves no unnecessary tensions or restrictions. In considering its relation to running efficiency these should be the only criteria.

Air resistance. As an athlete runs the resistance of the air not only requires him to do work which, in consequence, restricts his speed; it can also impair his running position; in particular, at top sprinting speed or when running into a strong head wind, air resistance tends to straighten the trunk. Under such circumstances, therefore, he maintains balance by shifting his Centre of Gravity sufficiently far forward

---

* Conversely, the rotary motion of the forearms, feet and lower legs may be considered *responsible* for the direction of ground reaction.

a   b   c   d   e   f

Figure 131

to counteract the tendency to rotate backwards. He leans well forward into a strong head wind and is more upright with a following wind. The need for greater emphasis on horizontal force when air resistance is increased has been mentioned already (page 39) and is illustrated diagrammatically (Fig. 30).

Head. By virtue of its weight (approximately a fourteenth of the total mass of the body in an adult) and position on the spine, movements of the head can have considerable effect on other parts of the body. Hence the expression 'The head is the rudder of the body'.

As a general rule it is better for the balance of the runner for the head to be kept in natural alignment with the shoulders, with the eyes directed to that end. However, a twisting of the head (i.e. in a transverse plane) need not upset balance and may even be necessary, sometimes, in middle and long-distance running.

The effects of a poor head position are often to be seen towards the end of a race, when runners are tiring; throwing it back straightens the trunk and shortens the stride.

Expenditure of energy

For practical coaching purposes the techniques of athletics are best studied through the concept of momentum (see also page 44), since accurate measurement of total mechanical work in athletics is always difficult and is frequently

Figure 132

impossible. For this reason, physiologists prefer to analyse in terms of energy, calculating directly from the amount of heat produced during exercise, or indirectly from oxygen consumption and carbon dioxide elimination. Although physiological techniques do not fall within the scope of this book, none the less they are closely related to the mechanics of running; the following information should be useful to coaches and teachers as a background to their study of man, the running machine.

As energy expenditure in running increases with the speed, there can be no optimum running speed. It has been calculated* that the rate of oxygen usage in an average sprinter running 'all out', provides energy at the rate of 13 horse-power, used up as follows:

Air resistance	0·50
Work against gravity	0·10
Positive acceleration of the limbs	1·68
Negative acceleration of the limbs	0·67
External work done	2·95
Overcoming muscle viscosity	2·25
Wasted in recovery	7·80
Total	13·00

In all forms of running some energy is spent on working against air resistance; as a man runs he drives part of the air to one side, and either carries along or pushes more of it in front of him. This requires work, diminishing his kinetic energy and, therefore, his speed. The force of this air resistance varies as the square of the runner's speed and is therefore greatest in sprinting. It has been estimated that, in still air, at a speed of 35 ft per second (the top speed of a good sprinter) the force of air resistance is about 3·58 lb.

When an athlete runs, his Centre of Gravity undulates continuously. Off the ground it moves up and down, and while he is in contact energy is used to stop the downward movement of the Centre of Gravity and to give it upward movement again. Because the foot makes contact with the ground almost directly below the Centre of Gravity, the retardation of downward movement can be expected to exceed the following upward acceleration, which occurs when the Centre of Gravity is in front of the foot. If this is so, the time spent in retardation is less than that of acceleration.

When the athlete is not in contact with the ground the vertical movement of his Centre of Gravity is, of course, regulated by the force of gravity. Here, again, the periods spent in upward and downward movement are most probably unequal.

Much more total energy is expended in producing and destroying the

* M. Grace Eggleton, *Muscular Exercise* (Kegan Paul, Trench, Trubner and Co. Ltd., England, 1936), page 273.

kinetic energy in the limbs. Each foot is brought to rest about every fifteen feet and the remainder of each leg is slowed down and speeded up in a continuous cycle of movement. In addition, as the movement is mainly rotary, the direction is continually changing. This means that there is a continual change in the momentum of the legs, and this also applies to the arms.

While the athlete has contact with the ground, part of this total change in momentum is produced by the work done by the driving leg, and accounts for much of the energy expended by this leg. However, when there is no contact with the ground, all change is produced by the transference of momentum from one part of the body to another, at the expense of energy; for there is always a loss of energy in any transference of momentum, because some is transformed into heat.

In consequence, if the work done by the driving leg is not equal to the expenditure of energy during all the movements of a running stride, the runner will slow down. This should serve to emphasise the danger of wasting energy through unnecessary movement and lack of proper relaxation.

Leg speed in sprinting is not limited by the neuromuscular mechanism. The mass of the leg, its moment of inertia in recovery, the rate of development of kinetic energy, internal viscosity, the weight of the athlete and the angle of propulsion—these are the limiting factors.

At very high running speeds, especially, muscle movement is extremely uneconomical (see also pages 31–3); in fact, the efficiency of muscular contraction approaches only 25 per cent. By its very nature, therefore, human locomotion must be wasteful. Yet, through superior balance, relaxation and timing, trained runners can undoubtedly conserve energy and transfer momentum from one part of the body to another, so improving their efficiency. Indeed, the skill accomplished in many sports consists largely of concentrating momentum where it is wanted without unnecessary waste of kinetic energy.

In contradiction to Professor A.V. Hill's original hypothesis* that the fastest time for a given middle or long distance could be attained by running at a constant speed, some physiologists have since suggested that the second half of such races should be run faster than the first, with the athlete conserving his anaerobic (i.e. oxygen debt) reserves until comparatively late in the race.

This latter opinion appears to have been substantiated, practically, in the running of many 1500m/mile races so far. But world records have

* A. V. Hill, *Muscular Activity*. Baltimore, U.S.A.: Williams and Wilkins, 1925.

been established with slower and faster first halves; and, quite often, an athlete has achieved good results either way on different occasions. The present inconsistent pace-pattern over these middle distances is not easily explained.

In all other men's running events, however, clear patterns have become established. Thus, all great 400m/440 yd races of recent years have been run at near-maximum pace, with the first half within 1.0 sec. of the athlete's best 200 m/220 yd time; yet without his slowing down by more than 1·0–1·5 sec over the remaining distance. In general, today's fastest 800 m/880 yd races are being achieved with the first half 5·0–7·0 sec slower than the runner's best-ever 400 m/ 440 yd time, and with the second half of the race, usually some 2·0–4·0 sec slower than the first.

Again—and almost without exception—fast 3 mile/5000 m races are now run with the first half 2·0–5·0 sec faster; with a very gradual, even, slackening of pace from beginning to end. And the pattern for 6 mile/ 10,000 m events is much the same, with the first half 10·0–20 sec faster than the second.

On the running tracks, then, it is not yet proven that the husbanding of anaerobic reserves is preferable to running with a uniformly accumulating load of oxygen debt. The writer thinks it very probable that Professor Hill's conclusion is still valid.

Hurdling and Steeplechasing

It is impossible to excel in hurdling and steeplechasing events without basic sprinting or middle-distance running ability. For these races are won mainly on the ground, and therefore the best method of clearing a hurdle or water jump is that which returns the athlete quickly to the track with a rhythm and effort akin to a running action. Hurdling and water jump techniques are therefore modifications of running form.

Hurdling

To avoid jumping—which checks forward momentum and interrupts the running action—good performers at these events clear the hurdles by using a running step-over action of the front leg, combined with a sideways-swinging rear leg movement. In clearing low hurdles (as in the 200 metres hurdling event) neither movement is greatly emphasised; but in the men's 110 metres race, where the barriers are 3 ft 6 in., even a tall, long-legged athlete has to exaggerate them (Fig. 133). The technique of the 400 metres (3 ft) hurdler falls between these two extremes.

The expert hurdler therefore runs over the obstacles mainly by 'making room' with his legs, and in the process raises his Centre of Gravity only a little more than in taking a running stride. Thus, in comparison with their times on the flat, champion high (3 ft 6 in.) hurdlers need no more than about 2·0 secs to clear ten barriers—an average of 0·2 sec per hurdle. Indeed, a few exceptional hurdlers have taken even less time.

Clearance: the flight-path of the Centre of Gravity. The fastest hurdle clearances are those where the athlete's Centre of Gravity is raised only slightly more than in taking a running stride—theoretically, with the high point directly above the obstacle and with take-off and landing distances almost equal (Fig. 134a). (Note that even in a running stride the take-off exceeds the landing distance, i.e. relative to the high point of the Centre of Gravity.)

However, in negotiating the obstacles, hurdlers are compelled to raise their Centres of Gravity even higher, and take-off distances are greater because:

(i) their approach speeds do not permit the close take-off shown in Fig. 134*a*; they need more distance in which to raise the leading leg; and by taking off farther away, in consequence, must spring higher to avoid dropping on to the hurdle. The Centre of Gravity therefore attains a higher point, in front of the obstacle (Fig. 134*b*);

(ii) although even 3 ft 6 in. hurdles can be cleared with the upper body and hips no higher than in running. this can be achieved only through a higher raising of the hurdler's Centre of Gravity; for, with the raising of the legs, the hips drop in relation to the Centre of Gravity (see page 57). If the Centre of Gravity were not so raised, the athlete would hit the obstacle.

Of necessity, therefore, even a highly-efficient clearance takes longer than a normal running stride. The distance it covers is also greater, and this, with the take-off to landing ratio, varies from athlete to athlete and, for any one hurdler, from one clearance to another. Distances and ratios are dependent upon:

(i) *economy of the clearance position.* In efficient high hurdling, a pronounced forward trunk lean and correctly timed arm and leg movement provide a 'lay-out' of extreme economy (Fig. 135*a*). Here the Centre of Gravity is as near to the hurdle as possible for a quick return to the ground. Conversely, a poor 'lay-out' (Fig. 135*b*) wastes time in the air;

(ii) *height of the athlete in relation to the height of the hurdle.* Compared with a taller athlete (where both are built proportionately and are equal in all other respects), the Centre of Gravity of a short hurdler moves greater vertical distances and therefore takes more time to rise and fall. In consequence his take-off and landing distances are greater.

He will not be at this disadvantage, however, if (e.g. through abnormally long legs) his Centre of Gravity is the same height above the ground at take-off. Using the same approach speed in both instances, an athlete should cover less ground in clearing a low hurdle than a high one;

(iii) *approach speed.* Theoretically an increase in sprinting speed lengthens both take-off and landing measurements. In fact, however, as a hurdler gathers speed over the first few flights so, successively, are increases in take-off distance matched approximately by landing

Figure 133   a   b   c

reductions; ratios change, but the overall distance is constant to within a few inches.

Conversely, as speed is lost (as usually happens towards the end of a race) take-offs shorten and landings lengthen. All this suggests that greater approach speed, with the concomitant lengthening of the take-off measurement, permits a more horizontal drive and a lower, faster clearance;

(iv) *leading leg action*. The faster the pick-up of the leading leg, the closer can the athlete get to the hurdle and the quicker his clearance can be. (This assumes a set speed of approach.) Accomplished hurdlers use a very fast, high leading leg action; flexion at knee and ankle reduces its moment of inertia about the hip joint, allowing maximum angular velocity; and its quick, high movement imparts speed to the hurdler's Centre of Gravity (Fig. 133*a*).

Through the sluggish action of a longer, heavier leading leg, tall hurdlers sometimes squander their height advantage; their take-off is too far back, with the Centre of Gravity raised too much in consequence. Tall men have the edge in these events, yet, through quicker, more exaggerated movements, athletes of a mere 5 ft 8 in. have demonstrated exceptional efficiency in clearing even high (3 ft 6 in.) hurdles. Often, the short hurdler's difficulty lies much more in having to stride unnaturally between the obstacles.*

A combination of fast, high leading leg action, forward lean (marked in high hurdling) and powerful thrust from the take-off leg gives speed to the Centre of Gravity in a more forward direction;

* But modern synthetic track surfaces have certainly helped shorter hurdlers with great sprinting speed, while adding to the difficulties of very tall, fast, long-striding athletes.

d   e   f   g

the efficient hurdler drives *at* the obstacles. In this way, athletes of only fair sprinting ability often maintain good average speeds throughout their races;

(v) *attaining the correct point of take-off.* A hurdle can be cleared efficiently only when the point of take-off is commensurate with approach speed, the subsequent raising and lowering of the Centre of Gravity and quickness in front of the obstacle; and it must be reached without overstriding.

If too close, the hurdler has to jump high to avoid the obstacle, getting his high point beyond it (Fig. 136*a*). If he is too far away (Fig. 136*b*) again he must jump high to avoid dropping on to it. Either way, he wastes time, is too erect, hurries the trailing leg, lands heavily and disturbs his sprinting rhythm.

A slightly shortened stride immediately prior to take-off encourages a good forward drive and body-lean, and can lead to a desirable (if only slight) forward rotation of the whole body before leaving the ground. (See also page 144.)

Although a hurdler running the 110 metres event in 13·4 secs has an average speed of only 26·8 ft per second (18·2 m.p.h.), at top speed in the race he might clear the hurdles at as much as 32 ft per second, i.e. 21·8 m.p.h. The formula $d = \frac{1}{2}gt^2$ (see page 16) can be used to calculate the time taken for his Centre of Gravity to rise specific distances, i.e. from take-off to the high point, and on this basis to estimate its horizontal motion in that time. Thus, at 32 ft per second:

Raised 2 in., it covers 3·3 feet
,,   3 ,,   ,,   4·0 ,,
,,   4 ,,   ,,   4·6 ,,
,,   6 ,,   ,,   5·7 ,,
,,   8 ,,   ,,   6·5 ,,

High | point

a

Higher | point

b

Figure 134

a

b

Figure 135

But these figures do not represent take-off distances, for at the instant of leaving the ground the hurdler's driving foot is approximately 1 ft behind his Centre of Gravity (measured horizontally), and his high point of clearance is in front of the obstacle.

In Fig. 137 it has been assumed that, in raising his Centre of Gravity six inches at a clearance speed of 32 ft per second, the high point is 1 ft in front. The take-off distance (A–D) is therefore 7·7 ft (i.e. 5·7 ft (B–C) plus 1 ft (A–B) plus 1 ft (C–D)). As to the landing (D–E); ignoring wind resistance (i.e. assuming a constant clearance speed), this will be fractionally less than 4·7 ft (i.e. 5·7 ft (C–E) minus 1 ft (C–D)); for, through a more erect landing position, his Centre of Gravity will not quite fall to its take-off level (Fig. 137).

To summarise: it is impracticable to lay down precise distances and ratios. In good hurdling:

(i) the Centre of Gravity's high point is as near, horizontally, to the hurdle as possible and is raised little above a normal running position. Controlling factors, here, are leading leg speed at take-off and the economy of clearance position. Thus, the hurdler spends the shortest possible time off the ground;

(ii) the hurdles are cleared at maximum horizontal speed. Therefore, provided condition (i) is fulfilled, the greater the distance between take-off and landing, the better. *In assessing clearance efficiency, time and distance should always be considered together.*

While hurdling events favour tall athletes,* short (5 ft 8 in.–5 ft 10 in.) skilful hurdlers lose less time in clearance than is often supposed, for, to some extent, they make up the disadvantage of an initially lower Centre of Gravity by using a closer take-off.

Figure 136   **a**   **b**

* The average height of the competitors in the 110 metres event in the 1968 Olympic Games was 6ft. Given exceptional sprinting ability, it is still possible to be under this height and a hurdler of international calibre.

Clearance: other aspects. The following features of leg action are basic to all good hurdling:

(i) a pronounced *forward* take-off drive (Fig. 133*a–b*);

(ii) a wide separation of the legs immediately after take-off (greatly assisted by a forward trunk lean (Fig. 133 *b–c*);

(iii) a fast leg-pivot (i.e. the front leg's downward-backward motion co-ordinated with the lateral recovery of the rear leg, Fig. 129*d–f*);

(iv) a landing which flows smoothly into the first of the running strides. The hurdler 'comes down running' (Fig. 133*g*).

In all four phases, front and rear leg movements should be regarded as components of a single action. In this respect, the important points are:

Timing of leg action. Ideally, the legs should move fast and continuously throughout clearance, and should be so timed that the front foot lands only slightly ahead of the Centre of Gravity (as in running) with the greatest possible backward speed relative to the hips (Fig. 133*f–g*). However, as the leg-pivot cannot begin until the front foot is clear of the hurdle, in high hurdling (and with short hurdlers particularly) there must be a split-second pause after take-off to allow the front foot to get into position for downward movement (Fig. 133*b–c*).

Pivot speed is influenced by horizontal speed, and the time spent off the ground. The greater the horizontal speed, the sooner can the front thigh begin its downward movement and the more delayed, relatively, can be the rear leg recovery. Other things being equal, an athlete with high clearance speed is capable of a better pivot timing than a slower hurdler—and obtains a smoother transition into the sprinting action.

A fast pivot, i.e. one related to the cadence of the running action, is the ideal, but this is possible only when the hurdler spends little time in clearing the obstacles. However, the pivot must always be properly

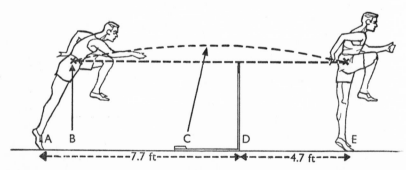

Figure 137

co-ordinated; if it is too fast for the rise and fall of the Centre of Gravity, the front foot lands too far behind the body and the athlete stumbles into a shortened first stride; if it is too slow, he may fail to clear the rear leg safely, or will land with the front foot too far ahead, checking his forward motion.

In general, a delayed rear leg gives faster and more continuous action, subsequently, and better timing and speed on landing. In fact, an efficient downward front leg movement is largely dependent upon the correct timing of the rear leg; a conscious attempt to 'claw' with the leading foot is not recommended. The holding of a forward trunk lean encourages and simplifies this delayed rear leg movement.

Absorbing reaction. The leg movements of hurdling are the cause of greater upper body twisting reactions than in normal running. Yet, these reactions can be channelled and absorbed without upsetting balance and running continuity—a simpler problem for flexible athletes.

At take-off the reaction to leg movement is shared between the ground (which reacts by driving the hurdler forward and upward) and the upper body (which absorbs reaction to the eccentric leg thrust— i.e. in a transverse plane—by its forward lean and pronounced arm action). (The so-called 'double-arm action' is contrary to efficient body mechanics, and is not recommended. For the writer regards it as an unnecessary and difficult modification to natural arm-leg co-ordination which, despite the claims made for it and its use by some champions, is *not* essential to good balance and lay-out over the obstacles.)

However, the body alone can absorb reaction to leg movement originating in the air; and here, action and reaction are in parallel planes, and possess equal and opposite angular momenta about an axis (of displacement) passing through the hurdler's Centre of Gravity.

As the leading leg moves down and back and, simultaneously, the rear leg recovers laterally (Fig. 133*d–f*), reaction is absorbed:

(i) *in the transverse plane* (Fig. 119*a*), by holding a forward lean, to increase the horizontal distance between the axis of displacement and the secondary axes of the shoulders (see also page 109). Thus, the arms, swung wide of the body to increase their moments of inertia, take up more reaction than would otherwise be possible. This lean also increases the trunk's moment of inertia about the axis of displacement, enabling the upper body to absorb any further reaction without markedly twisting out of sprinting alignment;

(ii) *in the frontal plane* (Fig. 119*b*), by lowering an extended 'opposite arm' in its backward swing, whilst simultaneously raising the

143

other, so preventing an exaggerated upper-body tilt towards the rear leg; reaction to counter-clockwise leg movement is absorbed by clockwise arm movement, and vice versa;

(iii) *in the sagittal plane* (Fig. 119c) by a straightening of the upper body. In this plane the legs may be considered to work in opposition; the 'unjacking' of the body is caused only by the action of the front leg, for the other perhaps encourages a weak *contrary* rotation, weak because of the rear leg's smaller moment of inertia about the Centre of Gravity (through which the axis of displacement must pass).

Because of the trunk's greater moment of inertia about this axis, both range and angular velocity of the trunk are far less than those of the leading leg rotating in an opposite direction. Moreover, while the leading leg movement blends with, and is quickened by, an overall forward body rotation (due to an eccentric thrust at take-off), this same rotation acts in opposition to the trunk's reaction. Therefore, although the trunk does straighten to some extent, nevertheless it maintains a forward inclination for balance and acceleration on landing. (See also page 104.)

Steeplechasing

In the course of running 3000 metres, clearing twenty-eight 3 ft hurdles and seven water jumps, and in terms of energy expenditure, the steeplechaser cannot resort to the crisp, exaggerated hurdling movements of the shorter races. However, as steeplechasing standards improve, so does the general efficiency with which the hurdles are negotiated.

It must be emphasised that the proper hurdling of the twenty-eight 3 ft hurdles is more efficient than clearances where the leading foot is placed on top of the hurdles. This latter method may be necessary for those who cannot hurdle but, since the athlete must raise his Centre of Gravity much too high and interrupt his running action, it is uneconomical. And it is slower, as is very obvious when a 'hurdler' and 'stepper' clear the last three or four hurdles in a close race. The would-be specialist steeplechaser should therefore master hurdling techniques.

In taking the water jump (Fig. 138) the skilled performer speeds up several strides before take-off and gauges this spot without chopping or changing stride (Fig. 138a). For it is essential to accelerate beyond average racing speed in order to negotiate this wide (12 ft) obstacle.

He then springs on to the rail, meeting it just above the hollow of the front foot (Fig. 138b). Now, by maintaining a crouch position over

144

Figure 138

a bent leg, he reduces the body's moment of inertia about the supporting foot, thus pivoting quickly and easily forward. The leg thrust (primarily horizontal) is powerfully yet smoothly co-ordinated (Fig. 138*c*). The trunk straightens, the rear leg is kept trailing momentarily and the arms are raised laterally for balance correction (Fig. 138*d*). The landing (about 2 ft from the water's edge) is made on one foot (Fig. 138*e*) and the first stride is taken on to dry land (Fig. 138*f*).

Experience proves that although, in the early laps, it is possible to clear the water in one leap from the rail, this becomes increasingly costly in terms of energy as the race proceeds. It is therefore more economical to negotiate the obstacle in the manner described, and to do this throughout the race.

Jumping (High, Long and Triple)

The laws of mechanics are the basis of a complete understanding of all modern jumping techniques and a knowledge of these laws is an essential foundation of ability to coach these events.

High-jumping

Spring (which can account for approximately 90 per cent of the height obtained) and lay-out are the key factors in this event.

In good high-jumping, the running approach improves vertical spring and provides horizontal motion for crossing the bar. The take-off movements impart, of first importance, vertical speed to the jumper's Centre of Gravity; secondly, they initiate most of the rotation required for lay-out. The greater his effective spring, the higher will a jumper raise his Centre of Gravity; but he must so combine horizontal and vertical movement, and adjust his point of take-off, that the high point of the Centre of Gravity's path is directly over the bar (Fig. 12).

Since the use of weights is not permitted by the rules, the modern high-jumper does nothing to disturb the flight curve of his Centre of Gravity (see pages 20 and 55); but by changing position in relation to it he can clear a higher bar. However, in the best jumps the Centre of Gravity's high point above the bar and the completion of lay-out coincide; and, of course, the athlete gets into and out of his lay-out without knocking the bar down,

Spring and lay-out are the key factors—yet maximum efficiency in one can be obtained only at the expense of the other. All good high-jumping, is therefore a compromise; to obtain economy of lay-out (though never *absolute* economy) good jumpers drive eccentrically at take-off (see pages 69 and 96), slightly reducing their effective spring, but in the process gaining more through their position over the bar. By contrast, poor high-jumpers, anticipating their movements in the air, sacrifice too much spring for their lay-out, or cross the bar in poor positions.

APPROACH. (1) *Direction*. The direction of approach can greatly

146

influence the component rotations at take-off, and their proportions about the vertical, transverse-horizontal and medial-horizontal axes (see pages 77 and 89). Indeed, the approach is so bound up with the jumper's take-off and subsequent movement in the air that, once habitual, any drastic change to it can mar performance.

An angled approach (i.e. from the side) can be advantageous to all high-jumpers, regardless of style, because (i) it facilitates a greater range of free leg swing at take-off (for the bar is not then at right angles to the jumper's line of approach), and (ii) it makes possible the throwing of some part of the body over and below the bar before the Centre of Gravity reaches its high point, of particular importance to jumpers employing a fast approach, who therefore need more *time* in which to clear the crossbar correctly.

However, when the angle is too acute, the athlete travels too much along the bar, at greater heights knocking it off at one point despite clearing it at another. An additional danger is that the lay-out will be anticipated at take-off, exaggerating the lean towards the bar and reducing effective spring. The recommended angle is one of approximately 20–30 deg.

One seldom sees a completely frontal (i.e. 90 deg. angled) approach, though many fine jumpers commence from the front before curving in to the bar on the last few strides—done naturally to direct the free leg at take-off and initiate rotational movements required for lay-out. Jumpers who employ a more frontal approach tend to attain the high point of their jump in front of the bar; often, too, their free leg action has to be restricted or modified.

(2) *Speed*. The importance of approach speed increases with (i) the raising of the bar, and (ii) a sharpening of the run-up angle (for then the jumper is inclined to be longer over the bar); it is greater in those styles in which the athlete (as distinct from his Centre of Gravity) crosses at an angle—as, for example, in an Eastern Cut-off (Fig. 139), or Fosbury Flop (Fig. 146).

In the sense that a ball, rolling horizontally, changes direction on an inclined plane, run-up speed in high-jumping cannot be converted vertically; nor, in this respect, should the take-off leg be likened to a stiff pole. For although, initially, the take-off leg straightens, with its foot well in front of the hips, it flexes immediately strain is put upon it (Fig. 99). In fact, were it straight and stiff throughout, it could contribute little thrust, because knee joint extension would then be impossible, and the jar would be tremendous.

147

Yet the speed of a high jumper's approach *does* have a definite material influence on his spring from the ground; for an increase, here, in controlled speed can contribute to an improvement in the *eccentric contraction* of the extensor muscles of the jumping leg (i.e. in the *speed* with which those muscles are *forced* to lengthen, momentarily), developing maximum tension and a greater pressure between the jumping foot and the ground (see also pages 31 and 32).

Dyatchkov* maintains that an increase of 0·1 m/sec linear speed increases the pressure on the jumping foot by 26–35 lbs which (with a maintenance of the take-off angle) can improve jumping height by approximately 3.5 cms. He gives former World record-holder Valeriy Brumel's approach speed as 15·65 m.p.h. at the penultimate stride.

In all good jumping the take-off foot is placed in front of the athlete at a distance which gives his free leg (in particular) and arms *time* to assist the thrust from the supporting leg (Figs. 99 and 140*j*); with greater approach speed, this foot must be planted even farther forward.

This demands, initially, a backward lean, and a lower hip position; and (*provided the jumper is strong and fast enough to use it*) it leads to a more favourable pre-spring position.

This long-striding, low, preliminary position is best obtained as a result of either (a) a comparatively slow beginning, with the body pitched forward in a semi-crouch and with the hips and legs 'moving ahead' of a relaxed upper body on a marked acceleration over the last three strides, or (b) a rapid increase in speed from the start, with less acceleration before take-off (Fig. 140).

* V. M. Dyatchkov, *High Jumping*, Moscow, 1966.

Figure 139

The value of the run-up to spring, therefore, lies in contributing to range, force and speed beyond what is attainable in a standing high jump. Jumpers should experiment to see if they can benefit from a faster run-up; yet each will possess a 'critical speed'* beyond which take-off efficiency will be impaired, varying greatly from jumper to jumper, largely because of variations in strength and intrinsic muscular speed. For most good high-jumpers a run of only a few effective strides is necessary. The majority of champions use from seven to nine.

TAKE-OFF. Here, the jumper must (i) impart maximum vertical velocity to his Centre of Gravity commensurate with (ii) acquiring just sufficient body rotation (i.e. total angular momentum) for his lay-out subsequently.

(1) *Attaining maximum vertical velocity.* A jumper projects himself into the air by moving his limbs so that he exerts a force against the ground larger than that supporting his weight; and the reaction to this additional force accelerates him upwards. His vertical velocity also depends upon the *time* this extra force is applied, i.e. the *impulse* (see page 36); the greater the impulse, the greater the velocity.

In a high-jump take-off, the free leg and both arms are first accelerated upwards against the support of the jumping leg (and, therefore,

d   e   f

against the resistance of the ground). Then, with the Centre of Gravity over the jumping foot and already moving upward, an additional impulse is applied through vigorous extension of the trunk and the

* Which can be improved, by training. Since increases in strength involve changes in *timing*, skill practice should accompany physiological modifications; skill-training and strength-training should go hand in hand.

Figure 140

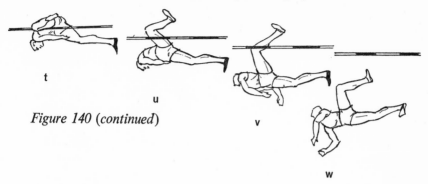

t

u

Figure 140 (continued)

v

w

take-off leg (Figs. 99 and 140). The important points, here, are:

Vertical Velocity (ft per sec)	Height (ft)	Time (sec)
5·66	0·5	0·177
8·0	1·0	0·25
9·8	1·5	0·306
11·31	2·0	0·354
12·65	2·5	0·395
13·86	3·0	0·433
14·97	3·5	0·468
16·0	4·0	0·5

(i) By bracing his take-off leg, initially, the jumper develops extremely powerful, if short-lived, tensions in the extensor muscles of the jumping leg—*eccentric contractions* (see page 32). And he must possess great strength in that leg—otherwise it will tend to collapse in reaction to the abrupt checking of his forward movement and the acceleration of the free leg and arms.

(ii) It is the *vertical acceleration* of the free leg and arms (*not* the mere fact of their upward movement) which invokes an upthrust from the ground. Here again, it is the athlete who makes the effort to change velocity and the ground which provides the reaction to the change.*

(iii) Fig. 141 illustrates the importance of *early* free leg speed. When a line drawn through the Centre of Gravity of (1) the thigh and (2) the foreleg and foot (and, therefore, of the Centre of Gravity common to both) makes a 30 deg. angle with the downward vertical

* E. F. Housden. 'A study in velocities; an analysis of the effects of the acceleration of the free leg in various athletic events' (*Coaching Review*, March 1966, Royal Canadian Legion).

(Fig. 141*a*) the *vertical component* of its velocity is already 50 per cent of its actual velocity; as much as 71 per cent of its actual value when that angle is 45 deg.! (Fig. 141*b*.) Through its downwardly-directed centrifugal effect, early free leg speed can also add to the pressure on the jumping foot.

(iv) To obtain maximum acceleration of the *whole* of the free leg *in the desired vertical direction* many good high jumpers straighten this leg as early as possible in its swing; but the knee is not kept locked (against a natural tendency to bend) once past a horizontal position.

☐   Centres of gravity of (1) thigh and (2) foreleg and foot

✗   Centres of gravity of right leg

Figure 141

Ideally, the free leg and arms should be moving at their maximum vertical velocity at the instant of take-off; for their acceleration afterwards cannot add to the athlete's velocity (see pages 20 and 55). (Hopper* suggests, however, that in good jumping the swinging leg ends its upward acceleration when horizontal. It then slows down, changing a downward thrust against the ground into an upward pull.

* B. J. Hopper. 'Comment' (A.A.A. *Coaching Newsletter*, No 21, April 1962, Amateur Athletic Association, England), page 8.

He affirms: 'The fact seems to be that the proficient jumper is able to time the extension at hip, knee and ankle with the changing upward acceleration of the free limbs, so as to develop at all times the maximum ground reaction that each muscle-group of the take-off leg can handle in turn.') *This points to the need for great strength in the extremity of the take-off leg, and in those muscles (rarely strengthened sufficiently) which might enable the free leg to accelerate beyond the horizontal* (see also page 38).

(v) The movements must occur as simultaneously as possible; otherwise the take-off impulse suffers (see page 38) and, because of the force of gravity, the free leg and/or arms (and, therefore, the Centre of Gravity of the whole body) lose velocity before contact with the ground is broken.

(vi) Maximum vertical velocity can be built up only when the accelerations of the different parts of the athlete's body take place over sufficient range of movement; this applies particularly to the actions of the legs.

(vii) The jumper's Centre of Gravity should be projected from the greatest possible height; at the moment of leaving the ground, the jumping leg and trunk should be fully extended vertically; and, ideally, the free leg and arms should be as shown (Fig. 99).

(viii) To attain maximum vertical velocity, the up-thrust from the ground must pass through the athlete's Centre of Gravity. Because of the need to initiate rotation at take-off, however, a *slightly* eccentric thrust is essential (see pages 66 and 69).

(ix) Throughout their rapid extension, the trunk and take-off leg must continue to exert the greatest possible effective force against the ground despite the upward movement of the rest of the jumper's body (see page 37).

(x) Too fast an approach gives insufficient time for the application of the various forces against the ground; vertical velocity is then reduced, as is the take-off angle.

(xi) The take-off surface must be firm, or the effect of the various body impulses will be reduced.

Fig. 142 shows the effect of ground reaction on a high jumper's Centre of Gravity (moving in a vertical plane). Here, the curve AB represents the low last stride before take-off (low, because of the importance of not wasting vertical impulse later (at B) in overcoming a dropping of body weight). BC denotes the path of the jumper's Centre of Gravity as this is influenced by a series of ground reactions while the jumping foot is on the ground. The arrows indicate the relative magnitudes and directions of these *residual* (i.e. ground reaction less body weight) forces at intervals of $\frac{1}{64}$ second.

In Fig. 142*a* ground reaction—through a series of controlled impulses —is always exerted at right angles to the direction in which the Centre of Gravity is moving, the effect being to change the latter's direction without changing its speed developed in the approach—excepting of course, a loss due to the rise against gravity. This, though ideal (postulating a jump much higher than the existing World record), is impractical.

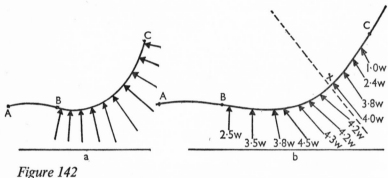

Figure 142

Fig. 142*b* shows what actually happens in a good jump, where the need is to build up one very large impulse in a very short time. Now, by means of a braced jumping leg and acceleration of free leg and arms (transmitted impulses) (see page 36) the Centre of Gravity is driven upwards by an average thrust of four times body weight. However, this is only achieved at the expense of Centre of Gravity speed (which, in this case*, dropped from 18·2 ft to 14·8 ft per second). In fact, the direction of ground reaction is unfavourable to the speed of the Centre of Gravity until point X is reached—when the forces of this reaction are rapidly diminishing.

A majority of take-off faults in this event are the result of anticipating movement in the air. Indeed, many errors in all forms of motor-learning are errors of anticipation. Good high-jumpers are 'take-off conscious'; poor ones over-anxious to cross the bar.

(2) *Acquiring rotation.* In even the best high-jumps the time between the instant of take-off and the moment when the body's Centre of

* B. J. Hopper. 'Rotation—a Vital Factor in Athletic Technique' (*Track Technique*, U.S.A., No. 15, March 1964).

Gravity reaches its high point is too short to permit an origin of lay-out in the air; it must begin on the ground.

For a given style of lay-out, however, the greater the jumper's spring, the less rotation he requires, for his rotation then acts for a longer period of time. For example, he will need less when projecting his Centre of Gravity 4 ft vertically (0·5 sec) than in raising it only 1·5 ft (0·306 sec). (See page 151.)

All three methods of acquiring rotation on the ground are combined in good high-jumping (see page 91). By checking linear motion (through momentarily fixing the take-off foot), transferring angular momentum (from the arms and free leg) and by thrusting eccentrically to the Centre of Gravity (with the jumping leg) a constant total angular momentum—in magnitude and direction appropriate to the style of crossing the bar —is developed on each jump. This can be resolved in terms of angular momenta about vertical, transverse-horizontal and medial-horizontal axes, which pass through the jumper's Centre of Gravity, at the instant of take-off. (Figs. 88, 90 and 91. See pages 80 and 89.)

With one exception, rotations about each of these axes can be acquired in all three methods. Thus, a high-jumper's free leg swing can impart backward rotation about a transverse-horizontal axis, rotate about a medial-horizontal axis, or twist about a vertical one; or, as usually happens, it can combine all three (Figs. 88 and 90). Arm action can produce similar effects; granted that the mass and length of an arm are considerably less than that of a leg—but many good high-jumpers swing *both* arms, and their rotational influence on the body is enhanced by virtue of the distance between their axis, the shoulders, and the body's main axis.

Again, depending upon timing, direction and emphasis, the thrust from the jumping leg can develop rotations about all three axes, or no rotation at all; and by momentarily fixing the take-off foot (i.e. by checking linear movement) a jumper can turn about a transverse-horizontal and/or a vertical axis (though, by this method, rotation about a medial-horizontal axis is not possible).

In building technique, the aim should be to select from the various alternatives according to (*a*) lay-out requirements, (*b*) angle and speed of approach and (*c*) the physique and powers of co-ordination of the athlete. For reasons of initiating rotations, Roll and Straddle jumpers spring from the leg nearer the bar, Scissor, Flop and Eastern Cut-off exponents from the outside leg. Each good jumper adjusts his run-up, to suit his particular interpretation of high-jumping form, his strength, speed, flexibility and neuromuscular co-ordination. A second important principle in the building of technique is to rely as much as possible upon the checking of linear movement for the rotational transfer required for lay-out.

In good jumping the approach angle is largely determined by the need for this and other forms of transfer—an angle of approximately 20–35 deg. for Scissor (Fig. 143*a*), Osborn Roll (Fig. 143*b*), Straddle (Fig. 140), Arch-straddle (Fig. 45) and Flop (Fig. 142) lay-outs, but somewhat greater (40–45 deg.) for most Eastern Cut-offs (Fig. 139). To develop maximum angular momentum, the free leg swings comparatively straight and accelerates through a wide range (Figs. 99 and 140).

a   b   *Figure 143*

High-jumpers who use a flexed free-leg swing (Fig. 146) are more dependent upon eccentric leg thrust and/or the checking of linear movement for their lay-out. For although a leg can swing with greater angular velocity flexed than straight, experience seems to prove that it cannot do so to the point of developing as much angular momentum, because of its reduced moment of inertia about the hip joint. (Nor, possibly, can it accelerate the jumper's Centre of Gravity over as great a vertical distance, keep him as long over his jumping leg nor privide as high a position of his Centre of Gravity at the instant of take-off.)

On the other hand, it would seem that a flexed free leg can the more easily be combined with a fast approach; and since (through a principle of neuro-muscular compensation which is said to operate through the entire range of human motion) the flexing of one limb encourages a simultaneous extension of its opposite, in all probability many high jumpers react instinctively to this natural tendency.

Those who can derive as large an upward impulse from the ground

156

by this means as others do using a straighter free leg must be able to hold their body rigid enough, momentarily, to transmit a large force in a very short time—a principle which applies, also, in good long and triple jumping.

Fig. 144 (a reproduction of film tracings) exemplifies the rotational origins and take-off patterns, in 1964, of Olympic finalist Diane Gerace (Canada), as viewed from the rear.

a   b   c   d   e   f

Figure 144

Straddle Take-off (Rear) (a–f) At the beginning of the take-off stride (*a*) the toeing out of the right foot suggests anticipation of weight-transference to the left. (*b*) Rotation about medial and longitudinal axes begins—both in the direction of the bar; the Centre of Gravity is now slightly to the left of the line of thrust, as viewed from behind and should remain so from here onwards. (But an excessive lean to the left will reduce vertical speed and the height of the Centre of Gravity at the instant of take-off.) (*c* and *d*) Body rotation about both axes is checked temporarily as the free leg takes up this angular momentum. (*e* and *f*) Trunk rotation about a medial axis is renewed as the free leg loses speed; and the trunk also takes over twist about its long axis and some backward rotation about a transverse axis. At this stage, the position of the free leg suggests insufficent early acceleration—and/or lack of flexibility—for it should be higher.

CLEARANCE. Once contact with the ground has been broken, the high-jumper (who is not permitted the use of weights) does nothing to disturb the flight path of his Centre of Gravity, the parabola of which has been determined previously by his approach speed and take-off spring. In the air, also, he possesses a constant total angular momentum about an axis of momentum (which passes through his Centre of Gravity) fixed in direction. This total angular momentum, usually, is expressed as (a) twist about his longitudinal axis with (b) gyration of that axis about his axis of momentum (see pages 114–19).

By altering the position of his body in relation to his Centre of

157

Figure 145

Gravity, however, he can clear a higher bar; and by changing his body's moment of inertia about the axis of momentum (with or without an interchange of angular momentum between twist and gyration) he can reduce or increase angular velocity.

Any movement he originates in the air must cause an equal and opposite reaction; clockwise action of one part of his body must produce a counter-clockwise reaction in some other part, and vice versa; but, within limits, the jumper can control the location of the reaction within his body.

The angular velocities of two moving parts of the body about their common axis, i.e. an axis of displacement (which also passes through the body's Centre of Gravity) are inversely proportional to their moments of inertia.

(For fuller details of the above-mentioned principles, see pages 20, 55, 80–119 and 146.)

(1) *Lay-out.* Fig. 145*b–j* illustrates a series of jumps (made from the left foot and observed from the pit side of the bar) taken by one athlete. The high point of his Centre of Gravity is the same each time (and is, correctly, directly over the bar); but, through adopting increasingly more economical positions about it, he is able to jump higher and higher.

Progressively, he reduces the gap between his Centre of Gravity and the bar; his best clearances are those where the bar has been raised to the level of—theoretically, even above—his Centre of Gravity. Put another way, the lay-out efficiency on each jump can be assessed by the body mass above and below the bar at this instant; the more mass

158

the jumper has above it, and the higher its position, the poorer is his lay-out. Conversely, the more mass there is below the bar at the high point of the jump, and the nearer it is to the ground, the better is his lay-out provided, of course, that all parts of his body eventually clear the crossbar.

Clearly, Fig. 145*b* position is of little value in jumping for height; and although the Scissor technique (Fig. 145*c*) is a considerable improvement, there remains a gap of approximately twelve inches between the bar and the jumper's Centre of Gravity; the upright trunk and raised legs force the seat down and there is little body mass below the bar.

By lying on his side at the high point of the jump an athlete using a Western Roll reduces the gap to approximately six inches (Fig. 145*d*); but there is little mass below bar level, and therefore the space between his Centre of Gravity and the bar is greater than it otherwise would be. An Osborn Roll (Fig. 145*e*) (i.e. with the back to the bar) is fractionally better, but there still remains little mass below the cross bar. (The many versions of the roll all possess at least some of the lay-out characteristics of these two main variations).

The bar can be moved even closer to the jumper's Centre of Gravity when he crosses on his back (Fig. 146*f*, Modified Scissors) or abdomen (Fig. 145*g*, Straddle); a complete lay-out in either style possibly saves as much as two inches on position Fig. 145*d*, but this lay-out has been unusual in a Modified Scissors jump.

When the trunk and limbs are curved round the bar, the gap is further reduced. Theoretically, such a position can be exaggerated to allow the jumper to pass over the bar while his Centre of Gravity passes beneath (Fig. 145*j*); however, this is not practicable in good high-jumping because it calls for the sacrifice of too much spring; and, of course, to 'jack' effectively the athlete would have to be moving much too slowly, horizontally, to clear the bar.

Fig. 145*h* illustrates the Arch-straddle, which incorporates the drap-

159

Figure 145 (continued)

ing effect and Fig 145*i* shows a very good Eastern Cut-off lay-out which achieves much the same efficiency; at the high point, the jumper's hips and abdomen are raised in relation to his Centre of Gravity as a result of the low positions of the head, upper trunk, arms and free leg. In either position (Fig. 145*h–i*) it is conceivable that the bar could be raised to the level of the Centre of Gravity's high point.

The importance of, and difficulty in, reconciling the essential upward spring and lay-out have already been emphasised (see page 146). Scissor jumps give good take-offs; the free leg movement is efficient and the body is kept over the jumping leg, but the lay-out is usually poor (Fig. 145*c*). A well-executed Eastern Cut-off combines the advantages of a Scissor take-off and an economical lay-out, but it requires exceptional control, suppleness and spring and is made even more difficult because the jumper must throw those parts of the body at take-off farthest away from the bar (i.e. his hips and legs) over first.

Hitherto, few athletes were happy in a Modified Scissor position (Fig. 145*f*), for control over the bar and safe landings* were difficult to achieve, though the style gives an excellent take-off. This, basically, was the form used by the 1968 Olympic Champion, Dick Fosbury, but with the bar crossed at approximately a right-angle (Fig. 146).

The Western Roll (Fig. 145*d*) provides a lay-out demanding no more than average co-ordination and flexibility, nor need it make exceptional demands on take-off spring. The Osborn Roll is better, but more difficult to control. A horizontal Straddle position (Fig. 145*g*) is better still, but take-off (i.e. rotational) difficulties are increased. An Arch-straddle (Fig. 145*h*) adds further to the problem of reconciling spring and rotation.

(2) *Movement originating in the air.* Even the best high-jumpers must

---

* The modern foam-rubber area makes landing much safer than it was, of course·

originate most of the essential turning movement at take-off, for there is so little time to do it in the air (see also page 154). However, certain minor rotations can be originated after contact with the ground has been broken—to the improvement of the jumper's take-off which, then, needs less of a rotational component. Movement originated off the ground, however, has its equal and opposite reaction within the jumper's body (see pages 98–119).

An outstanding example of this action-reaction is to be found in a well-executed Eastern Cut-off jump (Fig. 139). At take-off, through an eccentric thrust from the jumping leg and free leg swing, the jumper rotates backwards mainly about a transverse axis and, simultaneously, twists about a vertical axis.

At this instant, also, torsion at the waist is caused by a twisting of the hips and shoulders in opposite directions about the body's long axis—movements not in parallel planes, however, for the trunk is stretched on the side of the jumping leg and is compressed on the other side by the action of the free leg (Fig. 139a).

These movements are reversed in the air; the shoulders now twist in the direction of take-off, the hips again moving in opposition; the stomach is turned towards the bar. The lateral stretching of the trunk is also reversed (Fig. 139b–e). Thus, the rotation of the hip girdle, turning 'against' the upper body, brings the jumping leg to its horizontal position (Fig. 139e).

Again, the free leg, thrusting towards the pit, now acts in opposition to the head and shoulders which are momentarily forced below bar level. As a result of all these movements, the jumper attains an arched lay-out over the bar; his hips are raised in relation to his Centre of Gravity because of the low positions of his free leg, head, upper-trunk and arms (Fig. 139e).

Finally, at great speed, the Cut-off jumper lifts his head, upper body and arms 'against' a backward kicking of his free leg (Fig. 139f); otherwise (because of his body's overall rotation) he would strike the bar with his face or chest. He lands on his jumping leg and now faces the crossbar.

By comparison, Straddle and Flop jumpers originate less turning movement in the air and the styles certainly make fewer demands on co-ordination, timing and flexibility.

In the Straddle (Fig. 140) take-off rotation is again developed by an eccentric thrust from the jumping leg and transference of free-leg and arm angular momenta; rotation about a medial axis is marked, with some twisting about a vertical axis, both in the direction of the crossbar.

In comparing the various interpretations of the Straddle style, however, it would seem that rotation about a transverse axis is of a less uniform pattern; for whereas, in some Straddles, the angular momentum generated by the free leg swing and arms is more than compensated by the jumper's forward rotation about his take-off foot, resulting in forward rotation about this transverse axis, this is not the case in others, and the athlete therefore leaves the ground with backward rotation about this axis or no rotation at all.

It is suggested, however, that (in the horizontal plane), in general, the axis of momentum in a Straddle jump is at an angle 30–40 deg. to the bar, inclined (because of rotation about a vertical axis) slightly

Figure 146

The Fosbury Flop. Lacking the deliberate free leg and arm movements of the orthodox Straddle style, the Flop take-off impulse is probably less eccentric and the athlete's rotation due more to a sudden checking at the end of a fast, curved approach.

(*a-b*) The take-off originates a pronounced clock-wise rotation towards the bar and some twist about the body's longitudinal axis. (*c*) The lowering and trailing of the free leg and arms advances the upper body relative to the jumper's Centre of Gravity for an effective lay-out; and (*d*), through action-reaction, these leg and arm movements probably bring his transverse axis into line with his axis of momentum—so further twist is eliminated. Bent knees and arched back improve the lay-out and quicken the rotation; at the high point the Centre of Gravity is possibly at bar level.

(*e-f*) Finally, the lower legs are cleared, and the landing made safer, by straightening and lifting the legs 'against' a contrary motion of the trunk.

towards the pit. Throughout the jump, therefore, it is at a considerable angle to the jumper's longitudinal axis (Figs. 91 and 140), i.e. the cone described by the jumper's longitudinal axis about the axis of momentum is large.

After take-off (Fig. 140*p*) the jumping leg hangs momentarily, keeping the hips high in relation to the Centre of Gravity and so helping to advance the leading leg quickly over and beyond the crossbar (*important in all the high-jumping styles*). Then, to displace the trunk, in reaction, and so bring it more into line with the axis of momentum, the leading leg is swung back to a position more parallel with the crossbar; rotation and lay-out are thus speeded up.*

The head and chest barely clear the bar and drop rapidly below the main axis, while the hips and legs are raised above it (Fig. 140*t*). In addition, in some interpretations of the style, immediately after crossing the bar, the head and chest are forced even lower, against a downward thrusting of the free leg, to raise the hips and abdomen in relation to the Centre of Gravity and assist with the clearance of the rear (i.e. jumping) leg; this is then lifted and rotated (Fig. 140 *s–w*).

The reaction to these leg and hip movements momentarily checks or, if sufficiently strong, even reverses the twisting of the upper body. Finally, with the jumping leg clear, the whole body rotates uniformly, the arms and upper body coming to earth before the legs.

LANDING. As the high-jumper drops towards the pit he develops kinetic energy, and the greater the distance of his fall, the greater is that energy (see page 43). To reduce risk of injury the fall should not be too great and, on landing, he should lose kinetic energy as gradually as possible—hence the need for built-up, soft landing areas.

Where the jumper lands on his feet he should flex his leg (or legs) under control: but where it has to be made in some other way (Fig. 140*w* and Fig. 146*f*) the impact can be lessened—the force of landing per square inch reduced—by increasing the area of body contact; and where the kinetic energy is the result of considerable horizontal motion, rolling in the pit (in the same direction as that motion) also reduces the impact of landing.

Long-jumping

Theoretically a jumper who could raise his Centre of Gravity 4 ft at take-off (about the maximum achieved, so far, in high-jumping) and combine this with horizontal speed of 36ft per second (near the top

* An example of an inter-change of momentum, from gyration to twist.

163

Vertical speed (ft per sec)	Rise of C. of G. (ft)	Time of flight (sec)	Horizontal speed (ft per second)					
			25·00	26·09	27·27	28·57	30·00	31·58

1. Assuming the Centre of Gravity of the jumper rises and falls equally

5·66	0·5	0·354	8·85*	9·23*	9·65*	10·11*	10·62*	11·18*
8·00	1·0	0·500	12·50	13·04	13·63	14·28	15·00	15·79
9·80	1·5	0·612	15·30	15.96	16·69	17·48	18·36	19·32
11·31	2·0	0·708	17·70	18·47	19·30	20·22	21·24	22·35
12·65	2·5	0·790	19·75	20·61	21·54	22·57	23·70	24·95
13·86	3·0	0·866	21·65	22·59	23.62	24·74	25·98	27·35
14·97	3·5	0·936	23·40	24·42	25·53	26·74	28·08	29·56
16·00	4·0	1·000	25·00	26·09	27·27	28·57	30·00	31·58

2. Assuming the Centre of Gravity of the jumper 0·5 ft lower at the instant of landing than at take off

5·66	0·5	0·427	10·67	11·14	11·64	12·20	12·81	13·48
8·00	1·0	0·556	13·90	14·50	15·16	15·88	16·68	17·56
9·80	1·5	0·660	16·50	17·22	18·00	18·85	19·80	20·84
11·31	2·0	0·749	18·72	19·54	20·42	21·40	22·47	23·65
12·65	2·5	0·828	20·70	21·60	22·58	23·65	24·84	26·14
13·86	3·0	0·901	22·52	23·51	24·57	25·74	27·03	28·45
14·97	3·5	0·968	24·20	25·25	26·40	27·66	29·04	30·57

3. Assuming the Centre of Gravity of the jumper 1·0 ft lower at the instant of landing than at take off

5·66	0·5	0·483	12·07	12·60	13·17	13·80	14·49	15·25
8·00	1·0	0·604	15·10	15·76	16·47	17·25	18·12	19·07
9·80	1·5	0·701	17·52	18·29	19·11	20·05	21·03	22·15
11·31	2·0	0·787	19·67	20·53	21·46	22·48	23·61	24·85
12·65	2·5	0·863	21·58	22·52	23·54	24·65	25·89	27·26
13·86	3·0	0·933	23·32	24·34	25·45	26·66	27·99	29·46

* Distance covered given in feet.

recorded sprinting speed) could long-jump 36 ft—i.e. about 7 ft farther than the existing men's world record.

In fact, however, even the world's best long-jumpers take-off at less than 30 ft per second and raise their Centre of Gravity no more than 2½–3 ft. Even an athlete capable of a 7ft high-jump and a 9·3 seconds 100 yards sprint would be compelled in long-jumping to take off at horizontal and vertical velocities much less than might be expected. For, assuming he moves his Centre of Gravity 5 ft horizontally with his jumping foot in contact with the board, at a horizontal velocity of 36 ft per second, his jumping foot would be on the ground only 5/36 second, whereas a study of slow-motion films of 7 ft high-jumpers in action shows they need approximately $\frac{1}{5}$ second to impart an initial vertical velocity of 16 ft per second.

Efficient long-jumping, like good high-jumping, is therefore something of a compromise. In terms of a competent jumper's sprinting and high-jumping performances, neither speed nor spring are at a maximum: he reaches the board at a high, but not his top, speed, giving sufficient time for a great (but not his greatest) vertical impulse. In fact, it has been suggested that the proportion of horizontal to vertical take-off velocity in good long-jumping is very approximately 2:1.

The table on page 164 (which does not allow for air resistance) gives the horizontal distances travelled by the Centre of Gravity in flight for different combinations of horizontal and vertical velocity. Horizontally, the figures are based upon uniform sprinting speeds of 12·0 secs, 11·5 secs, 11·0 secs, 10·5 secs, 10 secs and 9·5 secs per 100 yards; vertically, upon the raising of the Centre of Gravity 0·5 ft, 1·0 ft, 1·5 ft, 2·0 ft, 2·5 ft, 3·0 ft, 3·5 ft and 4 ft. The times taken for the Centre of Gravity's rise and fall are also shown. *In estimating the length of a jump from these figures, one must allow for the distance of the Centre of Gravity in front of the board at the instant of take-off, and its distance behind the heels at the instant of landing.*

Horizontal speed (ft per sec)	*Height (ft)*							
	0·5	1·0	1·5	2·0	2·5	3·0	3·5	4·0
25·00	12 45′	17 45′	21 24′	24 43′	26 51′	29 00′	30 55′	32 37′
26·09	12 14′	17 03′	20 35′	23 48′	25 52′	27 59′	29 51′	31 31′
27·27	11 43′	16 21′	19 46′	22 53′	24 53′	26 57′	28 46′	30 24′
28·57	11 12′	15 39′	18 56′	21 57′	23 53′	25 53′	27 40′	29 15′
30·00	10 41′	13 30′	16 23′	18 45′	20 47′	22 35′	24 40′	25 39′
31·58	10 10′	14 13′	17 15′	20 01′	21 50′	23 42′	25 22′	26 52′

(Among others, the formulae used in preparing these tables are:

$$h = \tfrac{1}{2}gt^2 \qquad v^2 = 2gh \quad \text{or} \quad v = gt)$$

The table above shows the take-off angle (to the horizontal) made by the flight path of the Centre of Gravity at the instant of leaving the board, for varying combinations of approach speed and height of jump. The greatest practical angle must always be much less than 45 deg. (the angle sometimes recommended because it is generally known to give a projectile (*in vacuo*) maximum range). Indeed, it is impossible to jump at such an angle without using a very slow approach, or by directing the take-off ground-thrust backwards, at the cost of considerable horizontal speed.

A jumper moving horizontally at 30 ft per second could leave the board at an angle of 45 deg. only if his vertical velocity were also 30 ft per second (see pages 20–4)—when his Centre of Gravity would be raised 14 ft above its take-off height and the jump would measure approximately 56 ft! Again, even if he combined this take-off angle with the ability to raise his Centre of Gravity 4 ft (i.e. at an initial vertical velocity of 16 ft per second), his jump would be only 16 ft!

APPROACH. Ideally, the length of the run-up in long-jumping should be determined by the athlete's ability to accelerate to top speed, taking an additional three or four strides to prepare for an upward leap from the board. Since research proves that, in making a maximum effort all the way, men sprinters attain this speed approximately 180 ft from the start, ideally the approach should be over 200 ft; indeed, since it can be argued that a long-jumper's maximum effort is required at the end of the run, not at the beginning, his initial acceleration might well be more gradual and his approach even longer.

In fact, the world's best long-jumpers to date have seldom exceeded 150 ft in their approach; most have used from 120 ft to 140 ft and a few have barely exceeded 100 ft. In general, it can be said that they have attained, perhaps, no more than 95 per cent of their top sprinting speed. In future, records may be broken by using longer approach runs.

TAKE-OFF. (1) *Attaining maximum vertical velocity.* The mechanical principles involved in long- and high-jump take-offs are identical; the emphasis at this stage should be on imparting maximum vertical velocity to the jumper's Centre of Gravity (see pages 146–54). However, in relation to high jumping, there are the following differences:

(i) In this event the athlete attains a very much greater horizontal speed and does not accelerate into his final take-off stride. Therefore, although initially he places his jumping foot well ahead of his Centre of Gravity, he does not adopt the long, low final striding position of the good high-jumper, for to do so would result in a drastic reduction of essential horizontal speed.

(ii) The long-jumper 'gathers' for his leap approximately three strides before reaching the board. He then adopts a more erect position (to enable his jumping foot to reach farther forward on take-off) and on the penultimate stride lowers his hips slightly. Although the pattern throughout good long-jumping is by no means consistent, these preparatory movements usually lengthen the penultimate stride and shorten the final stride from three to nine inches.

(iii) At take-off, the free leg is swung well flexed at the knee, for speed of action (Fig. 147*b*). However, his more erect position here gives him a shorter time in contact with the board—and, therefore, a reduced impulse in comparison with the high jumper. A slower approach would give more time but would be offset by reduced (*a*) eccentric muscular contraction due to checking and (*b*) horizontal take-off speed.

The best long-jumping take-offs are those where resistance to forward motion is minimised and, within limits set by the athlete's great horizontal speed, a maximum vertical impulse is directed through the Centre of Gravity; the flexed free leg, head, shoulders and arms are first accelerated upwards against a braced jumping leg before an additional vertical impulse is applied through a vigorous straightening of that leg (Fig. 147*a–b*).

(2) *Rotation.* Just as the reaction to the force of a runner's leg drive is directed eccentrically to his Centre of Gravity (i.e. in all three main planes, sagittal, frontal and transverse) so does this also apply to a long-jumper's take-off movements. And just as, for balance when running, clockwise and counter-clockwise moments about the athlete's Centre of Gravity in each plane must be equal (subject to the limitations mentioned on page 130), so is this true of take-off balance in this event.

Balance in the frontal and transverse planes presents fewer difficulties than balance in the sagittal plane, for the jumper finds the effects of eccentric thrust weaker and, therefore, so much easier to 'absorb' and control.

In the sagittal plane, however, there is a strong tendency to forward rotation due to the action of the legs in the run-ups, the pivoting over and beyond the jumping foot as it rests, momentarily, on the board, and the vertical component of the athlete's leg thrust as it acts behind the Centre of Gravity (Fig. 147 *a–b*).

Backward rotation is encouraged by the horizontal component of the jumper's leg thrust, its vertical component when acting in front of his Centre of Gravity, and a transference of angular momentum from his free leg swing (Fig. 147*a–b*).

His emphasis on each of these constituent motions, determines whether, in this sagittal plane, the jumper leaves the board with backward rotation, forward rotation or no rotation at all. It would seem that backward rotation can be obtained only by greatly exaggerating the length of the last stride, destroying essential horizontal speed. On the other hand, experience proves that a fast, efficient long-jump take-off produces either no rotation in this plane or—more often— some forward rotation.

FLIGHT. The mechanical principles governing the movements of athletes free in space have already been discussed in some detail (see pages 20, 55, 80–119, 157 and 158) and these apply equally to the flight of the long-jumper.

Without the use of weights (not permitted by the rules) he can do nothing to disturb the flight curve of his Centre of Gravity; both linear and angular momenta with which he leaves the ground remain constant in the air (ignoring air resistance). Obviously, therefore, the long-jumper cannot 'jet propel' himself in flight and any movement he makes can be concerned only with the efficiency and safety of his landing.

(1) *Landing position.* The best landing position for a long-jumper is one which extends the flight path of his Centre of Gravity as far as possible and provides the greatest possible horizontal distance between his heels and Centre of Gravity, yet without causing him to fall backwards on landing.

To some extent, these factors are incompatible. A jumper adopting the best position for a delayed landing (Fig. 148*a*) fails to gain maximum horizontal distance with his heels, because, in this position, his hips have receded in relation to his Centre of Gravity. Again, a position giving maximum distance (Fig. 148*b*) hastens the landing, because the

168

e f g h

Figure 147

hips are now lower in relation to the Centre of Gravity; and falling backward in the pit is made more probable. Lastly, a position which presents no danger of falling back (Fig. 148c) reduces the distance gained by the heels and brings the jumper to the pit earlier.

In practice, therefore, the best landing position in this event must always be a compromise; the legs are somewhat below the horizontal and the trunk leans slightly forward (Figs. 147g and 149); but the greater the jumper's horizontal speed, the more effective the position he can adopt without falling backwards.

It has been estimated that, for every inch the heels are kept up, a jumper will gain about an inch and a half; all jumpers are aware of the importance of keeping the legs up on landing, and yet in most good long-jumps the legs are dropped immediately prior to it, a fault usually attributed to abdominal weakness. However, since all parts of a jumper's body in the air are experiencing the same gravitational acceleration, this explanation cannot be correct; for here the legs are not being held up by muscles while other parts of the body are prevented from falling, as happens in hanging, with legs raised horizontally, from a beam or wall-bars; when not in contact with the ground, the athlete can adopt and hold postures which would otherwise be more difficult (page 50).

It is suggested that at this stage of the jump the legs are lowered for one or several of the following reasons: because (i) of forward rotation originated at take-off; (ii) the jumper modifies his position to avoid sitting back in the pit; (iii) by instinctively raising his head and straightening the trunk, dropping his legs in reaction, he *feels* he is delaying the moment of landing; and (iv) of the tension of the extensor muscles of the

169

c   b   a   *Figure 148*

body, which may be too great for his hip flexor and abdominal muscles; only in this sense can the fault be attributed to muscular weakness (see page 50, *Weightlessness*).

Even in the best practical landing position, however, it is unlikely that the jumper's heels will contact the sand beyond an extension of the flight curve of his Centre of Gravity* (Fig. 149)—if, indeed, he can get them even *that* far in front of his body weight.

Landing efficiency is increased in long-jumping when, immediately before contacting the pit, the arms are behind the jumper (Fig. 149), for he then adds to the horizontal distance between his Centre of Gravity and heels (see page 56), and when he lands he can then throw the arms vigorously forward to assist the forward pivoting of his body, transferring momentum.

(2) *Movement in flight.* The foregoing analysis of the problems of landing and rotation off the board provide the key to the kind of movement in flight of greatest value to the long-jumper.

If he takes off with excessive backward rotation, he should extend his body—'hanging' (Fig. 150*b–c*)—to increase its moment of inertia about a transverse horizontal axis of momentum and so slow down this

Figure 149

* P. McIntosh and H. W. B. Hayley, 'An investigation into the running Long Jump' (*Journal of Physical Education*, England, November 1952).

a   b   c   d   e

Figure 150

rotation. Then, immediately before landing, he should 'jack' at the hips and so increase his angular velocity, raising and extending his heels in relation to his Centre of Gravity (Fig. 150*d–e*).

With either no rotation or forward rotation off the board about this same axis, however, he will profit from movements which will rotate the body backwards. If he leaves the board with no rotation, by cycling his legs forward, his trunk will automatically turn backwards, for he cannot change his total angular momentum in flight.

With forward rotation off the board, the angular momentum generated by the forward rotations of his legs (and, to lesser degree, his arms) should exceed his total angular momentum; the jumper's legs and arms must develop sufficient angular momentum not only to 'take up' these rotations, but also to turn the trunk and hips backwards in the sagittal plane. But when these arm and leg movements cease, the original body rotation (which cannot be destroyed in the air) reveals itself (see page 111).

A majority of athletes using this 'running-in-the-air' or 'hitch kick' style employ a single-stride technique (Fig. 147); yet it must be open to doubt that this displaces body weight sufficiently about the jumper's Centre of Gravity. Usually,

Figure 151

he completes this single stride and attains his landing position too soon, rotating forward again before landing.

It would seem that an extra stride in the air would provide an even better landing position; two strides could give greater displacement, yet without bringing the jumper too quickly into his 'jacked' landing position. And, of course, theoretically, three strides would be better still, though no jumper has yet succeeded in completing three *full* strides in the short time between take-off and landing.

With forward rotation off the board, a 'sail' jumper (Fig. 151) speeds up the rotation; by 'jacking' quickly after take-off he reduces his moment of inertia about the axis of momentum and so increases his angular velocity. A 'hang' position (Fig. 150*b–c*) merely slows this forward rotation by increasing the body's moment of inertia. As in the case of the 'sail' jump, it does nothing to absorb or counteract rotation.

Because of their smaller moments of inertia the arms, even when fully extended, do not possess the turning effect of the legs. Yet, by virtue of the position of the shoulders—a secondary axis, in relation to the jumper's Centre of Gravity, the location of the main axis—the arms possess a considerable turning effect above the head, particularly where there is a maximum possible distance between the axes (Figs. 147*d–e* and 150*c–d*).

As the arms are lowered, however, their turning effect on the rest of the body weakens progressively; and if the athlete remains in a fully stretched position they might eventually encourage a forward body rotation. However, in practice, by the time the arms are nearing their lowest position the jumper has already 'jacked' in preparation for his landing; the sweep of each arm's radius of gyration therefore 'embraces' the main axis and continues its (now very weak) influence in favour of backward rotation of the whole body (see pages 109–13).

Certainly in the sagittal plane the legs are always the principal 'absorbers' of body-rotation in long-jumping; the arms—held wide of the body—have more to contribute to balance in the transverse and frontal planes.

The benefits of a hitch-kick can be exaggerated; men have jumped well without it. Yet, so far as is known, all the world's 26-ft or better, long-jumpers, to date, have employed this technique, although it has sometimes been combined with a 'hang'.

Triple-jumping

The mechanical principles relating to high and long-jumping are also fundamental to the triple-jump (Fig. 152*a–l*) although, of course, the technique of this event differs.

Figure 152

The distance gained in a triple-jump is largely dependent upon the horizontal speed which can be developed in the approach and the extent to which this can be controlled, conserved and evenly apportioned over all three phases—hop, step and jump.

But, on each phase, the triple-jumper must also gain sufficient height at take-off and support his weight on landing. The movements required for this are responsible for opposing horizontal forces of a size which depends upon his mass, velocity, Centre of Gravity angles at take-off and landing and skill. The resistance of the air also reduces speed.

As he cannot change his weight, govern air resistance to any significant extent, nor produce a good jump without maximum (controlled)

173

approach speed, he influences his overall jumping distance by controlling his angles of take-off and landing, by skilfully reducing the landing shock, and to a limited degree by driving horizontally on each take-off.

For the conservation of horizontal speed, ideally, the jumper needs a low-angled take-off and a steeply-angled landing, but these are incompatible: take-off and landing angles must always be approximately equal, particularly in the hop and step. Therefore, in the hop, for example, where a good jumper gains his distance mainly on approach speed, a comparatively low take-off angle favours conservation, while the acute angle at which he lands tends severely to check his forward movement.

To reduce this resistance, therefore, the expert triple-jumper moves his leading foot back quickly, in a 'pawing' action, immediately before landing to reduce its forward speed in relation to the ground (see page 58), lands with the greatest practicable angle between his leading foreleg and the ground, and then 'gives' at the hip, knee and ankle joints. Yet he must stress none of these movements at a cost, subsequently, of essential vertical speed. These principles apply equally to the step technique.

An analysis of slow-motion film showing twelve good triple-jumpers in action (some Olympic and world record-holders) has indicated a general pattern of technique for this event. In each of the phases average times of take-off and flight for these jumpers were:

Hop		Step		Jump		Totals		
Take-off	Flight	Take-off	Flight	Take-off	Flight	Take-offs	Flights	Total time
0·132	0·562	0·164	0·421	0·171	0·640	0·467	1·623	2·090

(seconds)

The analysis revealed that, without exception, all the jumpers were progressively longer in contact with the ground over the three phases—hop, step and jump—denoting a gradual reduction in horizontal speed. Again, without exception, in terms of time, all were longest in the air during the jump and shortest in the step. In fact, their jumping rhythms were never even. In our hypothetical average jump, for example, the jumper's Centre of Gravity would rise 15 in. in the hop, only 8½ in. in

174

the step and (assuming it 12 in. lower on landing than at the instant of take-off) 14 in. in the final phase. These figures also underline the difficulty of gaining height in the step and jump; for the average pressure of the foot on the ground after the hop would be 4 times that of the body weight; after the step, 3·8 times.

Yet this is not to suggest that coaches who advise on even rhythm—'ta, ta, ta'—and a successively higher flight are wrong. For in coaching the triple-jump one must teach a higher, longer step than the athlete would do naturally and instil the idea of increased effort from phase to phase. Knowing what actually happens in a good jump a coach may yet correctly tell his athlete to attempt something different—the art, as opposed to the science, of coaching.

The basic principle in the triple-jump is that no one phase must be stressed to the detriment of the overall effort. But there can be no precise ratio of distance between the hop, step and jump because of the differences in athletes (in speed, spring, strength, weight, flexibility, proportions, etc., etc.) Certainly, no triple-jumper apportions his effort in exactly the same way from one jump to the next! However, a 10:7:10 ratio has been found suitable for beginners (e.g. 14 ft 9½ in.: 10 ft 5 in.: 14 ft 9½ in. for 40 ft), while international performances suggest a 10:8:9 ratio for the much more experienced athlete (e.g. 20 ft 9½ in.: 16 ft 6½ in.: 18 ft 8 in. for 56 ft—i.e. with greater emphasis on the Hop and Step).*

Hop. Because of the need to conserve horizontal speed, an expert triple-jumper gains hopping distance mainly as a result of his approach speed; his jumping foot does not reach out as far ahead as in a long-jump take-off nor is his final leg thrust as vertical (Fig. 152*a–b*). He does not need the time in contact with the board to gain the impulse of the long jumper. He could hop higher and travel much farther in consequence, but only at tremendous cost to speed in the step and jump. In this first phase, in particular, restraint in the apportioning of height and distance (and, therefore, speed) is essential.

If he is to follow the hop with a balanced step of good length, the jumper must keep his body upright in this first phase, his head in natural alignment with the shoulders. To avoid a backward-rotating movement, some jumpers reverse their leg positions with approximately

---

* Eng Yoon Tan, 'Research into the Hop, Step and Jump' (N.C.T.C.A. 29th Annual Meeting. Published by 'Champions on Film', 303½ SO Main Street, Ann Arbor, Michigan, U.S.A.).

equal moments of inertia about the hips (Fig. 152c–d), while others drop and straighten the free leg and markedly flex the jumping leg in flight to obtain a hitch-kicking effect. To facilitate an 'active' landing on the hopping foot this reversing of leg position should be completed relatively late in flight, with the thighs ranging through a wide arc, the hopping knee waist high and the legs moving continuously; for if the leading thigh is lowered prematurely the jumper's Centre of Gravity will pass quickly over and beyond the landing foot and his supporting leg will be too straight. In consequence, the step phase will be hurried, weakened and shortened.

A jumper who 'waits for the ground' lands in a slightly lower position and with greater leg flexion—both favourable to a 'cushioning' of the landing and a pronounced forward-upward drive in the step. At the instant of landing the Centre of Gravity should be approximately 1 foot behind the front foot, yet not so far back that the leg 'buckles' as a result of the backward thrust of the ground. In fact, the heel lands first, but a good jumper will not be conscious of it; the landing will feel flat-footed. The free leg trails at this stage (Fig. 152e).

The primary function of the arms is to absorb reaction to the powerful, eccentric leg thrust at take-off, to keep the trunk aligned properly. But in so far as action and reaction are interchangeable factors (see page 28), vigorous arm movement in a sagittal plane can also contribute to the horizontal component of leg thrust on each take-off; and, the upward acceleration of the arms on each occasion can augment vertical velocity (see page 149).

Ideally, therefore, the arms should be swung vigorously backwards and forwards in the hop, passing close to the trunk; and this applies also to the step take-off. However, where a jumper leaves the board unbalanced, rotating in a transverse and/or frontal plane, he must then extend his arms wide of the body in an attempt to produce counter-rotations (see pages 111–13); and, to the detriment of his step take-off, he must land with them in this sideways position at the end of the hop.

Step. The figure for the average pressure between foot and ground in landing from the hop in our hypothetical average jump for the twelve experts, gives some indication of the effort required to overcome that pressure and yet acquire new velocity and an optimum take-off angle for an adequate step. With beginners the step is used merely to recover from the hop; they put the next foot to the ground as quickly as they can, and this fault is accentuated when the hop has been too

176

high or the landing foot has been placed too far in front of the body. On the other hand, world-class triple-jumpers rarely step shorter than 14 ft.

The key to developing a good step lies in the use of the free leg at take-off. Flexed, it should be swung vigorously until its knee is at least waist high; simultaneously, the other leg should drive hard down and back (Fig. 152*f*). Experience proves that in flight a jumper should 'float'; here again, he should 'wait for the ground to come up to him'; keeping his front thigh at least waist level with a relaxed lower leg 'pawing' out and back for an 'active' landing. The rear knee swings forward to a position beneath its hip (Fig. 152*g*).

It has often been suggested that this more vertical rear thigh position is easier than trailing it far behind between take-off and landing, for the reason that, otherwise, gravity 'pulls the leg down'. In flight, however, any body position relative to the Centre of Gravity can be difficult to maintain only by virtue of internal muscular tensions. Since gravity acts on all parts of the body with equal effect, there can be no other reason (see pages 15, 16, 50 and 169).

The step landing is the same as for the hop, except that some jumpers swing both arms to the rear before contacting the ground, in order to use a double arm movement in their jump take-off. This arm action is used, usually, with a hang technique. Too vigorous a backward movement of the arms, however, pitches the trunk too far forward for an effective jump; the athlete then falls, rather than springs, into the pit—with considerable forward rotation. The trunk is best kept as erect as possible at this stage.

Jump (Fig. 152*i–l*). Fundamentally, the technique in this final phase is that of the long-jumper, but in comparison, the triple-jumper is a shorter period of time in the air and has less horizontal speed on landing—if his hop and step have been executed correctly. Also, after the two previous phases the control of his jump is more difficult.

With less forward speed on landing, the triple-jumper is in greater danger of sitting back in the pit. Here, a little forward rotation (although never consciously developed in a good jump) might be to the jumper's advantage; he is also in greater need of movement which will help to pivot him forward over the fulcrum of his heels, i.e. an immediate and pronounced flexing of the legs on landing (reducing his moment of inertia about his heels) and a throwing forward of his arms, to build up and then transfer their momentum. When momentum is transferred mass × velocity of the part equals mass × velocity of the whole (see pages 94–6).

Sail and hang techniques are usually preferred to a hitch-kick, for the latter needs more time and control than are generally available. In both styles, the legs should be brought through well flexed at the knees before straightening, thereby reducing their moment of inertia about the jumper's Centre of Gravity, speeding up their movement and diminishing a trunk reaction which would otherwise mar the landing position (see page 100).

CHAPTER NINE

Pole Vaulting

An attempt to coach pole vaulting (Fig. 153) without an understanding of the underlying mechanical principles has been likened to trying to read without a knowledge of the alphabet. For by planting his pole the vaulter creates a hinged moment which converts primarily linear motion at take-off into angular motion (see page 91); and then, simultaneously and interdependently, one pendulum (the athlete) swings from his

Figure 153

Adapted from Bill Falk, *Fibreglass Pole Vaulting*, M-F Athletic Company Inc., Rhode Island, U.S.A.

hands while the second pendulum (pole and athlete) pivots about the base of the pole (Fig. 154).

The good vaulter co-ordinates the timing of these two pendulums,

179

projecting his Centre of Gravity high above his top hand just as the pole attains a near-vertical position (Fig. 153). However, in gaining height the expert does more than employ these two movements; he completes and improves the vault by executing a powerful, carefully-timed and well-directed pulling and pushing action, driving his hips and legs upwards (Fig. 153).

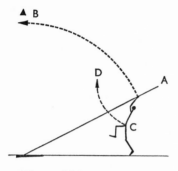

Figure 154

As Hopper has shown,* a vaulter's ability to clear a given height depends, first, upon his total angular momentum about a transverse axis through the point where the pole meets the box (Fig. 153). (In considering basic principles, the small mass of the pole and its moment of inertia will be ignored.) Second, it depends upon his skill in conserving and using that angular momentum properly.

The vaulter's total angular momentum consists of:

(a) his body's angular momentum about a transverse axis through his Centre of Gravity (due to the rotation of his forelegs in the run-up and, possibly, to rotational movement in the same forward sense in planting the pole), and

(b) the angular momentum of his Centre of Gravity, treated as a massive particle, about A (Fig. 155).

Figure 155

* B. J. Hopper. 'Rotation—a Vital Factor in Athletic Technique' (*Track Technique*, U.S.A., No. 14, December 1964: *Track and Field News*).

Pole Vaulting

As shown previously (see page 94) angular momentum can *also* be expressed in linear quantities; as the product MVR where M is the athlete's mass (supposedly concentrated at his Centre of Gravity), V his velocity, and R the distance between his Centre of Gravity and the box, measured vertically at right angles to his running path (Fig. 156a).

Assuming, for simplicity, uniform velocity in the approach and ignoring the slightly undulating path of his Centre of Gravity, then in equal times the latter moves through equal distances and its angular momentum about the box is constant. Geometrically, the areas swept out about A are also equal, each triangle having an area $\frac{1}{2}$VR (Fig. 156b).

The vaulter can add to this angular momentum at take-off by springing off the ground, substantially increasing R by this means (Fig. 155a); but for this to be advantageous he must plant the pole and jump without excessively checking his forward speed. (In all probability, all he can hope for is the *maintenance* of his run-up speed in the new direction.)

The vaulter's skill off the ground is the other basic factor. A successful clearance is largely dependent upon his ability to continue to move his Centre of Gravity forward and upward until it is vertically above A. After take-off, a large contrary turning moment (the product of his weight and its horizontal distance from the box) makes inevitable a gradual loss of angular momentum and tends to prevent this. It is therefore essential to reduce this horizontal distance as quickly as possible, particularly immediately after take-off.

Figure 156

The good vaulter achieves this by 'hanging' momentarily. He arches his body with the take-off leg almost straight (Figs. 155*b* and 153*b–d*)—a movement which (1) keeps his Centre of Gravity low and (2) permits it to move forward as rapidly as possible in a direction more horizontal than at the instant of take-off.

a   **b**   *Figure 157*

Just as the arm of a metronome oscillates more rapidly as its weight is moved closer to the fulcrum (Fig. 157 *a–b*), so, on leaving the ground, does the expert in this event give speed to his pole by extending his body momentarily, keeping his Centre of Gravity close to the pole's base. This exemplifies the principle of the conservation of angular momentum (see page 86), for by reducing the moment of inertia, angular velocity is increased proportionately.

Thus, the low trajectory of his Centre of Gravity reduces the distance R in the product MVR, and so V, his speed, is maintained (Fig. 155*b*). (The 'metronome effect' is illustrated in Fig. 157.) And, momentarily, he avoids making any downward motion on the pole through an upward acceleration of his body; it has only to bear his weight.

The immediate and pronounced bending of the fibre-glass pole assists both aims, reducing the shock of impact and loss of horizontal velocity. A wide grasp encourages this; it facilitates, simultaneously, a backward pulling action from a straightened upper arm and a forward thrust with the other—coupling movements which, while he is in contact with the ground, immediately establish the direction of pole-bend (Fig. 158) and, during the initial stage of the pole-borne phase, keep his body away from the pole.

Now, if the pole is to continue to turn about point A, the force exerted on it by the hands (in the illustration at a point near the top hand; in fact it will be somewhere between the hands and will vary)

Figure 158

must be directed slightly ahead of A so as to possess a beneficial turning effect (Fig. 159). The horizontal component of this force (HE) will be due to the equal and opposite checking (XB) of the vaulter's Centre of Gravity in this direction. The vertical component (HG) in the early stages of the vault should be little more than body-weight (Fig. 159*a*), for a marked upward acceleration at this time will increase the component and direct the resultant *behind* point A, slowing the pole down.

Figure 159

When the pole has moved more towards the vertical (Fig. 159*b*)—and with the vaulter's Centre of Gravity now approximately in line with the chord of the pole, i.e. an imaginary straight line between his upper grip and the bottom end (HA)—the direction of the force exerted through the hands (HF) will also have increased its inclination. Now, the horizontal (checking) force (XB) will be reduced, encouraging a premature straightening of the pole.

To avoid this, the vaulter begins an upward acceleration (i.e. his swing-up) without excessively reducing the pole's speed; the component (HG) is increased (Fig. 159b). And the more vertical the chord of the pole, subsequently, the smaller, progressively, will be the checking force and the better the position of the pole to support further upward accelerations.

In this swing-up the good vaulter 'breaks at the hips and knees', reducing the moment of inertia about his shoulders—so raising his body and increasing its rotational speed. Ideally, this should be delayed until it can merge, without pause, into the final pull-push actions. The swing-up reduces the speed of the pole-athlete pendulum, increasing the distance between the base of the pole (the fulcrum) and the Centre of Gravity common to pole and man.

From a position in which the hips and legs are close to and parallel with the pole (Fig. 153h) the good vaulter pulls *as the pole recoils*; for their simultaneous action can thus increase the impulse propelling him into the air (see pages 38–9). His body spirals upwards about a near-vertical axis, close to the pole, with the legs driven vertically in front of the plane of the uprights (Fig. 153h–k). The push is merely a continuation of the pulling action.

In these final moments the vaulter has not only to impart maximum vertical speed to his body; he has also to rotate it to raise parts of it still below the crossbar on releasing the pole (Fig. 153j–l). This he achieves partly by a transference of angular momentum acquired in dropping the legs *very slightly*, 'breaking at the hips' to assume an arched position at the high point (Fig. 153k). It is due mainly, however, to a couple (see page 68) created by the reaction to his thrust on the pole (acting vertically upwards) and the force of his weight (acting vertically downwards) (Fig. 57b). In efficient vaulting the force of the pole's upward thrust exceeds this downward pull; he releases the pole with his body rotating but still moving upwards (Fig. 153j–k).

Other aspects

Approach speed and height of grip. The following table illustrates how, other things being equal, the height cleared in pole vaulting is proportional to the take-off speed.

The speeds, expressed in terms of a 'flying' 100 yards run at uniform speed, are common to the event. The heights are *those above the position*

Speed		Height (to nearest in.)	
Seconds per 100 yd	= ft per sec	ft	in
9·8	30·61	14	7
9·9	30·31	14	4
10·0	30·00	14	1
10·6	28·30	12	6
10·8	27·77	12	1
10·9	27·52	11	10
11·0	27·27	11	7
11·1	27·03	11	5
11.2	26·79	11	3
11·3	26·55	11	1
11·4	26·31	10	10
11·5	26·08	10	8

(These heights have been calculated from the formula

$$\tfrac{1}{2}mv^2 = mgh, \quad \text{i.e. } h = \frac{v^2}{64})$$

of the vaulter's Centre of Gravity at take-off and take no account of the work he does in the later stages.

It has been assumed that all the kinetic energy developed in the run-up can be used in raising the Centre of Gravity whereas, in fact, some must be dissipated by the impact of the pole with the box, some by the backward thrust of the ground on the athlete's take-off foot and some in energy losses associated with the bending of the pole. In addition, of course, the vaulter must retain sufficient horizontal speed to cross the bar. It is beyond the scope of this book to attempt to assess any of these factors.

Greater approach speed will enable the athlete to use a higher grip, provided he has the strength to control the resulting increased centrifugal force of his swing (see page 46). A flexible pole can be held higher than a stiff one; and his height, weight, spring, skill, the direction and strength of the wind, the run-up surface, his general fitness and motivation—all will influence the height of the vaulter's grasp on the pole.

A vaulter should aim for a maximum effective grip (i.e. the distance between the top of his higher hand and the ground when the pole is upright in the box) equal to twice his standing height plus at least 24 inches. This can be used with maximum controlled speed at each height (which is recommended) or the vaulter can lower his grip and run slower at easier heights, progressively raising his grip and increasing his speed throughout a competition.

The fibre-glass pole gives greater height in vaulting than the bamboo and metal poles used previously because it permits the use of a higher grasp and, in bending markedly, stores more energy. However, because this energy must be restored to the vaulter—and *quickly*—at the proper time, he must select a pole appropriate to his weight, hand-hold and speed.

During the first decade of fibre-glass vaulting it was generally accepted that, because of the greater flexibility of the poles, good vaults could be made with the jumping foot within an area one foot forward or backward of a position under the top hand. Today's improved vaulting demands a greater precision—a return to the bamboo/metal pole concept whereby the foot should be *directly* beneath the top hand. For if it is further forward, or the plant too late, the modern vaulter—like the old—will be snatched prematurely off the ground.

The vaulting technique with bamboo and metal poles required the lower hand to be shifted closer to the top hand in planting; for with the hands no more than 6 inches apart the vaulter swung more effectively was less likely to turn prematurely, divided the work of his arms more evenly and could raise his chest higher above his grip on release, than with the hands wide apart.

With fibre-glass, however, a much wider hand-spread is used in the approach to control the higher grip, and even with a shifting of the lower hand in the plant (as some vaulters still prefer) a 1–2½ ft spread helps quickly to establish the direction of pole-bend (as has already been mentioned), keeps the body away from the pole during the swing, facilitates a fast raising of the legs in the swing-up and permits a more delicate adjustment of grip, as between one hand and the other; for slight changes in the suspension of body-weight can be made to control the degree of pole bend and its speed of straightening.

The swing. The 'hanging' movement (Fig. 153*b–d*) mentioned previously (page 182) is vital to bringing the pole to the vertical *only* when the highest grip is used commensurate with take-off velocity. With a lower hand-hold there will be neither the necessity nor time for such an extended body position.

Nor should it be exaggerated beyond the athlete's ability, later, to raise and flex his legs against gravity and the centrifugal force tending to tear him away from his grip. This is particularly true of the tall, long-legged athlete whose Centre of Gravity will be low relative to his grasp; he will develop greater centrifugal force than a shorter man swinging with equal angular velocity and will therefore require more strength and speed.

The swing-up. In the process of reducing the horizontal distance between himself and the box, initially (page 181) the vaulter will have maintained a low position of his Centre of Gravity—it has little vertical speed (Fig. 153 *b–e*); but now he must raise it quickly to retain, and even add to, the pole-bend and adopt a position from which he can benefit from its straightening and further increase his vertical speed by pulling and pushing. He lifts his legs viciously and rocks back, transmitting a large force through his hands into the pole (Fig. 153*g–h*).

To adopt and hold the best position from which to use the released energy when the pole straightens, the vaulter 'stays on his back', with knees, thighs and hips vertical, parallel with the pole (Fig. 153*h*). This must be no passive pose, however, for as the pole pivots and recoils the tendency will be for the legs to be driven down; the vaulter must try to bring his feet further and further above his head.

The pull-push. The good vaulter pulls as the pole straightens. Weaker, less co-ordinated athletes cannot pull against the pole's recoil and therefore delay their pull, doing less work and sacrificing height in the process. (See also 'Summation of forces', page 38.) The pull should be strong and fast, with the legs driven vertically in front of the plane of the uprights (Fig. 153*i*).

The turning of the body occurs partly as a result of a leg action whereby the original free leg is stretched vigorously upwards (vertically by some, and to the left of the pole, assuming a left-footed take-off, by others) while the take-off leg, flexed, cuts behind, turning the hips. It is also due to the unbalanced position of the hands, one above the other, which encourages a twisting of the shoulders in the direction of the grip. Turning (twisting) speed is related to pulling speed.

The push is merely a continuation of the pull.

The release. Ideally, all parts of the vaulter, and therefore his Centre of Gravity, should rise at maximum vertical speed until he has released the pole. Then he should 'jack' (i.e. flex markedly at the hips) to raise his abdomen in relation to his Centre of Gravity, improving his lay-out (Fig. 153*k*) (see page 55). Finally, with his hips clear of the bar, he should 'unjack' quickly to clear his head, chest and arms, depressing his abdomen and folding back his legs in reaction.

The more efficiently a vaulter converts horizontal to vertical movement, the greater the period of time for which he is over—and tending to drop on to—the bar, and the faster and more skilful must be his final movements.

Throwing

In all four throwing events the distance obtained is dependent upon the speed, the angle of release of the missile, and, in the discus and javelin events, certain aerodynamic factors.

Speed

An efficient throwing technique is one in which the athlete exerts the forces of his entire body over the greatest range practicable (force × distance = work; see page 43) and, therefore, for the longest period of time (force × time = impulse; see page 36); for the speed of release in throwing is proportional to the average force exerted through the implement's Centre of Gravity. Other things being equal, the greater total body force produces the greater speed and the longer throw, since force = mass × acceleration (see pages 25–7 (Newton's First and Second Laws) and page 36).

The forces must be exerted against the missile in the proper direction, however—so far as practicable, in the direction of the ultimate throw; for the total effective force in throwing is the sum—the resultant—of all the components of the various body forces acting in that direction. As a general rule, in throwing, however, in the preliminary movements there is more horizontal drive than lift, and in the delivery more lift than horizontal drive. The eventual effect is to release the missile at an appropriate angle to the horizontal.

These two principles are fundamental to correct preliminary movement in throwing—in the run-up, glide or turns. In good throwing they are exemplified in the fast stretching and powerful recoiling of large muscle-groups; in the driving of body weight from one leg to another and (in the hammer and discus events in particular) in the use of maximum radius of movement in the turns.

In particular, by driving the pelvis ahead of the trunk, the good thrower creates torque between hips and shoulders; active trunk muscle is stretched rapidly in an *eccentric contraction* which exerts maximum tension. (See also pages 31 and 32.)

The various forces of the body should be exerted in definite sequence and with proper timing; for the release speed in a good throw will be greater than in a bad one, even if the same effort has been expended and throws are equal in all other respects.

From a purely mechanical point of view it is immaterial in what order a given set of forces is applied, one by one or simultaneously; the final speed is the same. To accelerate a shot, discus, javelin or hammer, however, each body lever in turn must be capable of moving faster in a given direction than the missile is moving in the same direction; and the faster the lever can move the greater will be its effective force.

In a summation of throwing forces, therefore, the levers of the body should operate so that each can make a maximum, or very near-maximum, contribution to speed. Hence the use of slower but more forceful muscles and levers first (i.e. of the trunk and thighs); while the faster but relatively weaker joints (i.e. of the arms, hands, lower legs and feet) exert their forces after the missile has developed considerable speed. While the feet and hands *transmit* force during the earlier movements, therefore, their own smaller forces are *added* later (see *Impulse*, page 36).

However, there must be no undue delay in the application of the various forces because of forces which tend to retard the missile even before it leaves the thrower's hand, i.e. gravity (which tends to reduce upward motion) and the friction between the athlete and the ground at the instant of foot contact (which tends to slow the missile horizontally). Of major importance, also, is the need for maximum impulse. *All forces should therefore be applied as simultaneously as practicable.* (See pages 34 and 38, 71–7.)

Turns, glides and run-ups should be as fast as an athlete can use to good purpose; never so fast that he is unable to exert full body force subsequently in the delivery. In this respect, each athlete possesses his own 'critical', optimum speed of preliminary movement.*

For maximum speed of release the ground must provide adequate resistance to the thrower's movements, and for as long as he is in contact with the missile, for the force he can exert against it is limited, very largely, by the counter-thrust of the ground.

Fig. 160*a* and *b* illustrate how force in a horizontal plane can be

* Which can be improved by appropriate training.

a   b   *Figure 160*

lost when both feet are off the ground. As the athlete on the turntable
(Fig. 160*a*) attempts to put the shot, upper and lower parts of his body
rotate in opposite directions (Fig. 160*b*); reaction to his movement in
a horizontal plane must be absorbed by the turntable and his body,
not by the ground. Likewise, force applied vertically in throwing is also
dependent upon the resistance of the ground.

As Housden points out,* in developing angular momentum in discus
throwing the athlete must have some part of each foot or, at least the
whole of one foot, in contact with the ground. He recommends the
following experiments; first, stand with both feet on the ground and
with the right arm back behind the shoulder, swing the arm horizontally,
and as it comes to the front of the body, raise the right foot and rise
on the left toe. Through a transference of angular momentum from the
arm, the body will then turn in the same direction (see page 94). Then
stand with only the left foot flat on the ground, repeat the arm movement
and again rise on the toes. There is again a transference of angular
momentum. (Here, in the first instance, a couple is derived from equal
and opposite horizontally-directed forces exerted through the feet;
in the second instance, these forces arise at the ball and heel of the one
foot.)

In a third experiment, stand with only the ball of the left foot in

* E. F. Housden, 'Mechanics applied to Discus Throwing' (*Discobolus*, The Discus
Circle Magazine, England, No. 8, December 1959).

190

contact with the ground and repeat the arm movement. There will be no transference; (indeed, if the foot rests on a smooth surface, it will rotate towards the arm, in reaction, together with other parts of the body). From this, Housden concludes that a (right-handed) discus thrower is unable to increase his angular momentum from the moment his right foot leaves the ground in the back of the circle until the instant his left foot lands in the front of the circle, and both feet are on the ground again.

Certainly, a thrower can exert his greatest forces when both feet are firmly in contact with the ground (Fig. 180 *h–k*). In the shot and javelin events in particular, however, effective contact by the rear leg is broken once it has completed its drive, and contact with the ground is maintained only by the leading foot (Figs. 189 and 190). It is important to consider the timing of the breaking of this rear leg contact in relation to the movement of the arm, to see how continued maximum horizontal force can be applied to the missile.

Figure 161

Taking shot putting as an example; when the front foot comes to the ground (Fig. 161) it loses speed. The horizontal force exerted by the ground has then a two-fold effect: it causes both athlete and shot to rotate about this foot, and reduces the forward speed of the Centre of Gravity common to athlete and shot. This is illustrated diagrammatically in Fig. 161, where the continuous straigh lines shtow the couple causing rotation, and the dotted line represents the retarding force. (It should be noted that the two equal and opposite forces, F2, which balance and, consequently, do not affect the movement of the athlete, are used to clarify the illustration.) (See page 68.)

This sudden checking force causes an instantaneous change in speed at each point of the putter's body except one—below which all parts are slowed down, while all parts above this point are speeded up. It is important to realise that when the hand exerts a force on the missile, either above or below this special point, the reaction tends to move the feet forwards or backwards respectively. (When considering the move-

191

Figure 160

ment of a rigid body, this point is known as the *centre of percussion*, and its exact position can be calculated. (See Fig. 163.) As our shot putter is far from rigid, however, it can only be said that this point will be some distance above the Centre of Gravity.)

By way of illustrating this principle; when a man holds a shot with both hands at arms' length above his head and, after an upward jump, pushes the shot forward while he is off the ground, his feet should move forward (Fig. 162*a*); but when, under similar circumstances, he thrusts the shot forward at chest height, the reaction should then move them backwards (Fig. 162*b*). (By the same token, when the arm circling shown in Fig. 117 is executed at the level of the man's centre of percussion, his feet are unaffected and the movement invokes only the simplest of turntable reactions.)

In shot putting, correct technique requires the rear foot to be firmly in contact with the ground until the arm strikes (Fig. 189), permitting the ground to resist the tendency of the feet to move backwards. Once this rear leg has done its work and the arm strikes higher, however, the backward reaction on the hand tends to move the front foot forward and the ground reacts against it, allowing continued maximum force to be exerted.

Throwers who break contact with the ground before the missile leaves the hand may do so for lack of arm and shoulder strength; for a combination of the implement's inertia and accelerations developed by the legs and trunk may be too much for the arm — whose final action may have to be delayed until the accelerations have been reduced.

Or, again, contact could be broken prematurely to reduce the athlete's forward motion. Or the feet may be too close together or otherwise incorrectly positioned. Or the arm could be striking too horizontally. (See also pages 38 and 222.) On the other hand, a Russian view* of discus throwing is that coaches deal with men, not machines; that athletes strong in the oblique musculature of the chest and abdomen, but relatively weak in the legs, should release with both feet in contact; whereas those whose legs possess a high speed-strength quality will *naturally*—and from a position where the legs are somewhat closer together—jump at this stage, releasing with both feet off the ground.

Maximum release speed in throwing (*particularly in the shot, discus and javelin events*) *is influenced by the 'hinged moment' principle* (see page 91), whereby, on attaining maximum, controlled (i.e. 'critical') speed at the end of the preliminary run-up, glide or turns, the front foot is checked (Figs. 188, 189, 190).

As we have seen, the checking force at the foot is one of two equal parallel forces acting in opposite directions, producing a turning couple —a forward rotation, a 'hinged moment'. This checking force also reduces the forward speed of the Centre of Gravity common to thrower and missile.

As the speed of a point on a turning body is directly proportional to its distance from the axis (which, in this case, is the athlete's front foot) the throwing shoulder will now possess more speed than the Centre of Gravity, but whether or not it is greater than the thrower's original linear speed depends upon the extent to which the Centre of Gravity slowed down. This, in turn, depends primarily upon the horizontal distance between the Centre of Gravity and the front foot as the latter comes to rest.

In javelin throwing, where this foot is far in advance of the Centre of Gravity (Fig. 190e), most—if not all—parts of the athlete lose speed at this instant. In so far as there is rotation about the foot, all parts of his body above the Centre of Gravity may move faster but not as fast, perhaps, as his linear speed immediately beforehand.

Such a sacrifice is still worth while to the javelin thrower, however; indeed, it *has* to be made in good throwing. The front foot must be stretched well ahead of the body in order to provide an effective throwing position and, in view of the thrower's forward speed, to give sufficient *time* for the movements of throwing. The writer has seen no

* USSR Higher Scientific Research Institute of Physical Culture, 1970, 'Final effort technique in the Discus Throw' (reprinted in the *Yessis Review of Soviet Physical Education and Sports,* Vol. 5, No. 4, December 1970).

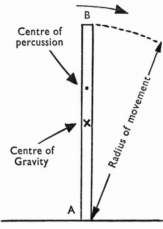

Figure 163

When the base of a rod (i.e. a thin, rigid, uniform rectilinear mass), moving horizontally in a vertical position, is brought to rest the speed of its Centre of Gravity drops by a quarter. If B is twice as far from A as the Centre of Gravity, it will move twice as fast as the Centre of Gravity; so the speed of B is improved by 50 per cent at the instant of checking. The centre of percussion in such a mass is always two-thirds AB from A. In a rigid non-uniform mass, however, the problem is very much more difficult.

mathematical evidence to show that a javelin thrower's upper body improves its linear speed as a result of the front foot coming to the ground, but if that speed is retained, or is only slightly reduced, while the athlete adds his powerful throwing movements, it is obviously of great advantage, subsequently, to the speed of delivery (see also page 225).

In the shot and discus events, however, where (in comparison with the javelin thrower) at this instant the front foot is not excessively in advance of the Centre of Gravity (and where, therefore, there is less checking of forward speed), it seems very likely that there *is* a point which corresponds to a centre of percussion, (Fig. 163), with parts of the body above it speeded up; but this point will be changing constantly with changes in body position.

In throwing, the force exerted is to some extent dependent upon the athlete's mass. In discus throwing, for example, as the arm strikes (Fig. 187e–h) the tendency is for the rest of the athlete's body (especially the throwing shoulder) to move downward and backward in reaction, so reducing the effective force and time/range over which force can be applied.

In good throwing, the reaction to the vertical component of the arm's movement will be counteracted by the up-thrust of the ground, regardless of the thrower's weight; but the reaction to the horizontal component will cause the upper-body of a comparatively light athlete to move backward more than a heavier thrower, other things being equal.

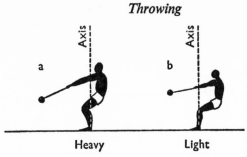

Figure 164

The heavier man can therefore exert more effective force over greater distance.

It follows that an athlete who breaks contact with the ground prematurely in shot putting will in all probability find the error more costly than when throwing a discus since, obviously, the reduction in delivery impulse involves the ratio of missile weight to body weight, i.e. the mass of the missile times *its* speed, equals the athlete's mass times *his* speed in an opposite direction. (See pages 29, 37, 190.) For this reason it has been argued that the reduction in delivery impulse due to breaking ground contact before the discus leaves the hand is little more quantitatively significant than a gun's recoil as a shell is launched.

Sheer mass is also of value in increasing the radius of movement in discus and (particularly) hammer throwing, increasing the missile's speed; for the balancing of the moments of weight and centrifugal force (previously referred to on page 79) will be maintained by a closer approach of a massive athlete's body to an axis passing through his feet than in the case of a lighter athlete (compare Fig. 164*a* with *b*).

It can be shown, however, that an increase in mass for the purpose of increasing the missile's radius gives diminishing returns—a point is soon reached where minute gains in this regard are offset by other factors, e.g. lack of speed or agility.

Angle of release

If a thrower is to obtain maximum distance, it will not be sufficient to give the missile maximum release speed; it must also be thrown at an appropriate angle.

When points of release and landing are the same height above the ground (*and aerodynamic factors may be ignored*) *the optimum angle for the projection of a missile, regardless of its speed is one of* 45 *deg.* (see page 22). In this case, vertical and horizontal component velocities

195

Figure 165

are equal, and the missile also lands at a 45 deg. angle. (Here, distance is as the square of the velocity; so, for example, if the velocity increases by 10 per cent (from, say, 100 to 110 units) the distance will be increased by 21 per cent (from 100 to 121 units).)

It should be noted that the weight of a missile reduces the *resultant* vertically upward thrust delivered to it. To release, e.g. a shot at this angle, therefore, a thrower must exert a force *vertically* greater by 16 lb-wt than the *horizontal* force.

However, in all four throwing events in field athletics the implement is thrown from a point above the ground and this affects the release angle. Then the optimum angle depends upon height and velocity of projection. In the shot and hammer events (where aerodynamic factors are of no account) the *optimum* release angle will be less than 45 deg. Theoretically, a missile thrown at this angle will land at an angle with the horizontal equal to the angle its release direction makes with

Figure 166

Height of Release in ft	Angle of Projection with horizontal (deg.)	Release Speed f.p.s.	Put in ft	in
8	45	44	67	8
		43	64	11
		42	62	2
8	40	44	68	0
		43	65	3
		42	62	7
8	35	44	66	7
		43	64	0
		42	61	5
8	30	44	63	9
		43	61	4
		42	58	11
7	45	44	66	10
		43	64	1
		42	61	5
7	40	44	67	0
		43	64	4
		42	61	8
7	35	44	65	6
		43	62	11
		42	60	4
7	30	44	62	7
		43	60	1
		42	57	9
6·5	45	44	66	5
		43	63	8
		42	60	11
6·5	40	44	66	7
		43	63	10
		42	61	2
6·5	35	44	65	0
		43	62	5
		42	59	10
6·5	30	44	61	11
		43	59	6
		42	57	1

the vertical. For example, a shot released at 41 deg. 40 min. will land at 48 deg. 20 min. (Fig 165) (released 7 ft above the ground, at a velocity of 41.3 f.p.s. for a distance of 60 ft measured horizontally from the point of release.)

197

Fig. 166 shows diagrammatically how, with just enough speed to attain a given distance from a specified height, the ideal angle can be found by bisecting the angle between a vertical line drawn through the thrower's hand at the instant of release, and a straight line joining this point and the point of landing. Fig. 15 shows that a low release speed requires a lowering of the release angle.

The optimum angles of projection for a put of 60 ft (measured horizontally from the point of release to the point of landing, i.e. not allowing for the distance between the inside edge of the stop-board and the hand (approximately 1 ft)), from release heights of 8 ft, 7 ft and 6½ ft, will be 41 deg. 12 min., 41 deg. 40 min. and 41 deg. 54 min. respectively.

In hammer throwing the missile is released so close to the ground relative to the distance thrown that, for all practical purposes, 45 deg. can be assumed the proper angle of delivery. More accurately, however, its optimum angle is always slightly *less* than 45 deg. because it is released about 5 ft above the ground. The precise angle can be calculated by first measuring the *distance thrown* and *time of flight* (to 0·1 sec) before referring to the graph (Fig. 167) on page 199.

If, for example, a throw of 60 m (196 ft 10¼in) takes 3 sec, optimum conditions will not have been achieved. At the point where the vertical, and horizontal lines (representing time and distance, respectively) meet, the sloping 35 deg. release-angle line and the 80·33ft/sec release speed-curve also intersect. If the missile is released at this speed, yet at an angle of 43 deg. (follow *the curve* upward and to the right) it will reach 63 metres (206 ft 8¼ in.)

The forces exerted in throwing give greater release speed when they are directed nearer to the horizontal. In fact, a study of the dynamics of shot putting reveals that within certain limits speed of release is more important to an athlete than the use of an optimum angle.

In theory, a shot projected 60 ft from a point 7 ft above the ground must rise to a height of 18 ft 9 in (Fig 165). Yet most 60 ft shot putters do not put so high and therefore do not release the shot at such optimum angles. It could be said, of course that by contriving to improve their elevation they could put even farther—and this could well be true of some. It seems likely, however, that at such levels of performance the factors responsible for maximum release speed conflict with those that give an optimum angle of delivery.

The table on page 197 illustrates the importance of release speed in these throwing events. The distances (to which, as we have seen, ap-

Figure 167

Relationship between distance thrown, time of flight, velocity and release angle.
After Fig. 2 of *Hammer Throwing*, Howard Payne, Amateur Athletic Association,
England, 1969; and Toni Nett's graph in his *Die Technique beim Stop and Wurf*.

proximately 1 ft should be added) have been estimated to the nearest
inch on the basis of three release heights ($6\frac{1}{2}$ ft, 7 ft and 8 ft) and four
angles (30 deg., 35 deg., 40 deg. and 45 deg.). They are based upon the
facts of dynamics, irrespective of the launching mechanism, human
or otherwise. Air resistance has been ignored.

These figures, calculated to illustrate a point developed by Professor

199

A. C. Aitken (University of Edinburgh), have been obtained from the following expression for the length of the put:

$$\frac{v^2 \sin 2a}{64}\left\{1 + \sqrt{1 + \frac{*\,64\,h}{v^2 \sin^2 a}}\right\}$$

where v = release speed, a = angle of projection and h = height of release. The table shows that:

(i) 40 deg. is nearer the average optimum angle than 45 deg;

(ii) from 35 deg. upward comparatively little increase is made in putting, for the same velocity;

(iii) an increase in height of release from $6\frac{1}{2}$ ft to 7 ft gives only an additional 5 to 8 in. in distance; from 7 ft to 8 ft only 9 to 15 in.;

(iv) relative increases in velocity very decidedly increase distance. For example, putting from a height of 7 ft, at an angle of 35 deg. at 42 f.p.s., an athlete attains 60 ft 4 in., but gains only 1 ft 4 in. by increasing his angle by 5 deg.; whereas, by returning to an angle of 35 deg. and increasing his speed by only 1 f.p.s. he gains 2 ft 7 in., and as much as 5 ft 2 in. for an increase of 2 f.p.s.

The proper use of the strong leg and trunk muscles in throwing plays a vital part not only in releasing the missile at maximum speed, but also in projecting it at a correct angle; in particular, where the angle is too low, leg and trunk action—and not the arm or arms—is usually at fault.

In fact the emphasis on 'lifting' the missile with the legs and trunk during the actual throwing movements should be considerable, especially where comparatively great horizontal speed has first been developed in the run-up or movement across the circle; for the angle of projection will be the product of the preliminary and throwing movements (Fig. 168).

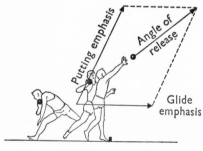

Figure 168

Aerodynamic factors

In discus and javelin throwing, distance depends upon the speed and angle of release, as with the shot and hammer events, but by virtue of their size and shape, aerodynamic forces also influence the flight of discoi and javelins. These missiles do not describe simple parabolic curves.

As yet, the aerodynamics of discus and javelin throwing have not been worked out in detail, for many unknown factors and variables (not the least variable of which is the thrower himself!) are involved. What follows is therefore no more than an outline of basic, relevant aerodynamic principles, with some comment as to their significance in these events.

General principles. In moving through the air a discus or javelin drives part of that air to the side and pushes some in front of it. This requires work and, therefore, a reduction in kinetic energy and, therefore, speed. The air's resistance depends upon the shape and size of the missile; generally, the thinner and sharper it is at the front, the smaller is the resistance—which can be further reduced if its cross-section narrows gradually towards the rear, giving a 'streamlined' effect.

In front of the missile, therefore, there is a region of increased air pressure, and in its path another region where the air whirls irregularly, causing diminished pressure (Fig.169). The kinetic energy of turbulent air movement in the wake of a discus or javelin accounts for much of the work needed to move it through the air; but the better the streamlining, the smaller will be this air disturbance. (Fig. 170; both bodies (*a* and *b*) present the same effective cross-section to the on-coming air yet, because of its streamlining, object *b* has 1/25 the specific resistance of *a*.)

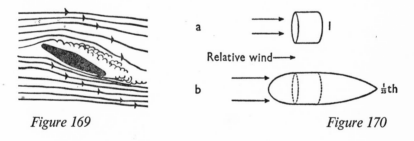

Figure 169   *Figure 170*

Air resistance is also dependent upon the speed of the discus or javelin, and is proportional to the square of the velocity.

When a missile is inclined at an angle to the wind (Fig 171) the resultant of the forces exerted upon it by the air can then be resolved into vertical (*lift*) and horizontal (*drag*) components. The ratio between lift and drag depends upon the *angle of attack*, i.e. the acute angle between the plane of the discus or javelin and the direction of the relative

201

Figure 171

wind (Fig. 172). Even small variations of this angle can sometimes produce abrupt alterations in the lift/drag ratio.

The term *relative wind* refers to the movement of the air in relation to the missile. *All motion is relative;* a discus or javelin can be suspended in an air-tunnel with the air flowing past, or it can be moving through still air. A following wind can therefore reduce the speed of the relative wind (lessening lift and drag) and a headwind can increase it (but must not be too strong to be of benefit in these two events).

A relative wind will not always directly oppose the flight-path of the missile's Centre of Gravity, however; usually, in throwing, air currents are continuously varying in both strength and direction. Nor, always, do the missile's flight-path and its plane coincide, an angle between being called the *angle of incidence;* this can

Figure 172

be positive (i.e. above the angle of the flight path) or negative (i.e. below that angle) (Fig. 173). The angle between the plane of the missile and the horizontal is called the *attitude angle* (Fig. 173).

Fig. 174 shows diagrammatically how the sizes of the various lifting forces acting on a discus are dependent upon the angle of attack. When the angle is zero the upward forces on the lower surface act only near

Figure 173

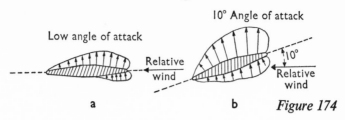

Figure 174

its leading edge; but as the angle increases (Fig. 174*b*) these forces also increase, both above and below the discus. When the angle is of a certain size, however, air turbulence forms along the trailing edge and grows markedly with a further increase in angle.

The shape of the discus or javelin and the angle it makes with the direction of the relative wind cause the speed of the air flowing over the missile's upper surface to be greater than that underneath. As a result, there is a diminished air pressure above the missile and the upward forces acting on it are greater than the downward forces (Figs. 169 and 174*b*).

All the forces of the air acting on a discus or javelin may be added together to form a resultant (see page 39) which acts at a point called the *centre of pressure* (Fig. 171). This changes position with a change in the angle of attack; as this angle increases, the centre of pressure moves forward and the resultant force increases. Conversely, with an increase in the speed of the relative wind, the centre of pressure moves farther back. There is a limit to which the angle of attack can be increased to advantage, and if that limit is exceeded turbulence behind the missile disturbs the smooth flow of air over its upper surface; the upward force (lift) almost disappears, drag increases and the missile stalls. This limiting angle is called the *stalling angle*.

The lifting force acting on a discus or javelin in flight therefore depends upon:

(i) its shape (which influences the nature of the air-flow past its upper and lower surfaces);

(ii) the angle of attack (within limits, the greater angle produces the greater lift);

(iii) the surface area (the greater the area, the bigger the total lifting force);

(iv) the square of the air speed (for example, lift is four times greater when a javelin is released at 50 m.p.h. than at 25 m.p.h.);

(v) air density (the greater the density, the greater the lift).

203

The Mechanics of Athletics

The flight of the discus. A discus (which experts think a comparatively poor aerodynamic design) 'performs most efficiently as an airfoil between speeds of 69·8 and 80 feet per second' (Ganslen*), and its spin, in good throwing, provides some gyroscopic stability in flight, keeping the lift/drag ratio relatively constant.

Relative wind

Centre of pressure

Figure 175

For all its gyroscopic benefit, however, spin itself tends to increase the angle of attack (Housden†)—a paradox which, perhaps again, shows how, in the analysis of athletic movement, advantages must be weighed against disadvantages. To illustrate: when a discus rotates in a clockwise direction (seen from above, Fig. 175) its left side meets the air at a greater speed than its right side; the former spins into the air, while the latter moves away from it. Therefore the upward force exerted by the air on the left side is greater and the centre of pressure is to the left. There is therefore a tendency for the discus to turn about the axis XOX' (Fig. 175) (clockwise, as seen from X).

This does not happen, however, because of its spin. Assuming an upward pressure exerted somewhere on OY (Fig. 175), this turns the discus about the axis OY (clockwise, as seen from Y); for each point on the missile is raised as it moves across OX and continues to rise until it reaches OX' (Fig. 175); every point on the discus is higher at X' than at X and, as a result, its front edge tilts upwards. Conversely, a downward force exerted at the centre of pressure will lower this front edge.

The following figures show estimated distances a discus can be thrown for given initial speeds, using combinations of projection and attitude angles (Cooper, Dalzell and Silverman‡ (Purdue University) from wind-tunnel data supplied by Ganslen). Here it has been assumed that spin stabilises a discus, in good throwing, to the point of main-

* R. V. Ganslen, *Aerodynamic factors which influence discus flight* (Research Report, College of Arts and Sciences, University of Arkansas, U.S.A., May 1958).

† E. F. Housden, 'Mechanics applied to Discus Throwing' (*Discobolus*, The Discus Circle Magazine, England, No. 8, December 1959).

‡ L. Cooper, D. Dalzell and E. Silverman, *Flight of the Discus* (Division of Engineering Science, Purdue University, Indiana, U.S.A. May 1959).

taining a constant attitude angle (the authors claiming that motion picture analysis indicates no appreciable change in this angle throughout flight).

The following conclusions may be drawn from these tables.

TABLE 1
INITIAL VELOCITY 70 f.p.s.

Projection angle

	15°	20°	25°	30°	35°	40°	45°	50°
10°	104	120	130	138	144	146	144	133
15°	110	124	136	144	150	150	148	136
20°	114	128	142	150	152	154	152	140
25°	114	128	144	150	156	154	152	144
30°	114	128	142	152	156	156	152	148
35°	112	128	140	148	154	154	152	144
40°	106	124	136	146	150	152	152	144
45°	104	120	134	142	146	146	146	140
50°	98	116	128	136	142	142	142	136

Attitude Angle (left axis label)

(Distances in feet)

TABLE 2
INITIAL VELOCITY 80 f.p.s.

Projection angle

	15°	20°	25°	30°	35°	40°	45°	50°
10°	132	152	170	178	186	186	182	172
15°	148	164	180	188	194	194	186	174
20°	152	172	188	196	200	198	194	178
25°	154	174	190	200	204	202	198	184
30°	154	170	188	198	204	204	198	186
35°	150	168	184	192	200	202	196	184
40°	144	162	176	186	196	198	190	182
45°	134	150	172	180	186	190	184	180
50°	128	148	166	176	180	180	176	172

Attitude Angle

(Distances in feet)

(1) *Speed of release is the factor of greatest importance,* as emphasised previously (see page 197, Shot Tables). A small increase in speed in discus throwing gives a comparatively larger increase in distance, however, because the lift on the missile is proportional to the square of its speed.

(2) *For a given speed, the most important variable is the angle of projection.* 150 to 200 ft throwers should project at 35 deg. to 40 deg.; throwers of lesser ability should increase the angle slightly, but never above 45 deg.

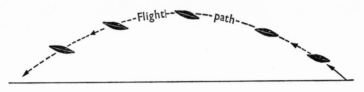

Figure 176

(3) *The attitude angle should be between 25 deg. and 35 deg.* At the instant of release, therefore, there should be a negative angle of incidence of approximately 5 deg. to 10 deg. Although, at such an angle, air pressure will tend to depress the front edge of the discus, the ascending half of its flight-path automatically reduces the angle (Fig. 176). If the latter tendency is the greater, then the missile moves gradually into alignment with the tangent to the path of its Centre of Gravity—presenting a considerable surface-area to the ground during the descending half of the flight, benefiting by the cushioning effect of the air beneath and, therefore, gaining distance through a gliding motion (Fig. 176).

On the other hand, a positive angle of incidence upon release must increase as the discus moves forward and its flight-path curves towards the ground (Fig. 177). In addition, air pressure increases this angle, leading to a progressively stronger resistance to forward motion and, eventually, stalling. (The stalling angle for a discus is said to be approximately 30 deg. (Ganslen*).)

The greater the speed of the discus upon release, and the stronger the opposing wind, the smaller should be the attitude angle as the discus leaves the hand, to avail the throw of a more favourable lift/drag ratio. Practical experience proves that a discus can be thrown farthest into a wind blowing from front-right (right-handed athlete), and

* Ibid.

Figure 177

Throwing

Pharaoh* (Great Britain; 4th, Discus, 1956 Olympic Games) maintained that the difference between throwing directly *into* a wind, and *with* that same wind, varied—for him—from about 5 ft for a wind-speed of 7 m.p.h. to approximately 15ft at 20 m.p.h., the greater distance being thrown into the wind. Stronger headwinds reduce stability in flight and therefore shorten the distance.

Flight of the javelin. From 1955 to 1961 javelin throwing world records rose primarily through the use of implements of improved aerodynamic design, giving an increased stability and a better lift/drag ratio in flight. They were considered to add as much as 25 ft to a good throw. These 'glider' javelins as they came to be called, were made in several different diameters to suit a thrower's ability and varying throwing conditions; they possessed a lighter spearhead, a more evenly-distributed surface-area and tapered less towards the tail than previously.

The year 1961 saw the end of this era of javelin throwing, however, because the International Amateur Athletic Federation further revised its specifications so as to limit these aerodynamic features and enforce a stricter uniformity as to the type of javelin used throughout the world. The javelin now permitted has a reduced diameter (a maximum of 30 mm as against the previous 35 mm) and its angle of taper and length of point are also specified. However, the regulations still permit some variation, for the javelin-diameter can vary from 25 mm to 30 mm and its Centre of Gravity can be between 90 cm and 110 cm from the point. Compared with the javelins used prior to 1955, in fact, the present implement remains 'aerodynamic'.

There is considerable disagreement and ignorance, even among experts, as to the behaviour of an aerodynamic javelin in flight, and little reliable scientific information on this subject at the present time.

A Russian opinion, that of V. L. Kuznetsov,† assesses the optimum angle of release for the modern javelin at 28 deg. to 30 deg., ideally with the shaft at this instant in alignment with the tangent to the path of its Centre of Gravity (i.e. with a zero angle of incidence). When this improved javelin is released at much greater angles (e.g. at approximately 45 deg., as necessary in throwing the 'old' design) the tendency is to give it too great an angle of attack. It then rises and falls abruptly, for its centre of pressure is too far in front of its Centre of

* M. Pharaoh, 'Observations on Discus Throwing' (A.A.A. *Coaching Newsletter* No. 4, April 1957, Amateur Athletic Association, England), page 9.

† V. L. Kuznetsov, 'Mastery of Javelin Throwing Technique' (*Track Technique,* U.S.A., No. 2, December 1960, *Track and Field News*), page 46.

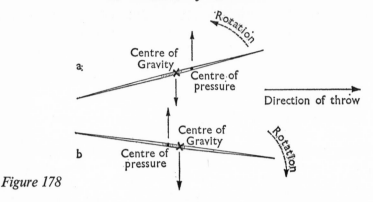

Figure 178

Gravity, creating backward rotation and stalling (Fig. 178*a*). (These two centres and the distance between them then create a couple whose turning effect is proportional to that distance (i.e. the arm of the couple).)

Some experts are of the opinion that the optimum release-angle of these aerodynamic javelins is nearer 40 deg., with an angle of incidence at this instant of approximately –10 deg.; but they admit that an athlete must be very skilful to use it without creating too great an angle of attack, for in attempting to produce more 'lift' in the delivery, the tendency is to raise the head of the javelin. It is easier to control this angle when the delivery is more horizontal, and most athletes prefer to 'play safe' in this way.

In an aerodynamically well-designed object the centre of pressure remains comparatively stable in flight; the relatively even distribution of surface-area of the modern javelin is said to reduce the motion of its centre of pressure as it travels through the air. The desired flight is one in which the Centres of Pressure and Gravity approximately coincide throughout the early stages. As the flight proceeds, and the angle of incidence increases, the Centre of Pressure moves back and, just prior to landing, causes the point to drop rapidly in the required landing attitude.

In the process of releasing a javelin a thrower automatically imparts spin about its long axis—the result of an outward rotation of his elbow and the sequence with which his fingers break contact during delivery (Fig. 179). This spin (clockwise, seen from behind, in the case of a right-handed thrower) can possibly give some gyroscopic stability in flight, provided it is of sufficient intensity. However, whereas some experts speak in terms of thirty revolutions per second in a good

a　　**b**　　**c**　　**d**　　**e**　　**f** *Figure 179*

throw, and regard this spin as important, others deny that much spin is ever developed or has any significance.

To summarise:

(1) *Again, speed of release is the factor of greatest importance* as in all other throwing events, and lift on the javelin is proportional to the square of its speed (as with the discus). Within limits, thinner javelins can be selected and used to reduce the drag factor.

(2) *The optimum angle of release for the 'aerodynamic' javelins* is probably between 35 and 40 deg.; the 'old' design of javelin was released at approximately 45 deg.

(3) *The attitude angle of the 'aerodynamic' javelin* at release should possibly be a little less than the release angle; the vital thing here is not to present too great an angle of attack to the relative wind. Then, in a good throw, the missile will reduce its angle to the horizontal slightly and maintain that angle until it begins to fall, when it again rotates forward to land almost flat, point first.

(4) *The gliding qualities of the 'aerodynamic' javelin* are especially valuable in the gaining of distance during the second half of flight.

Throwing techniques

Hammer. Technique, in good hammer throwing (Fig. 180), is designed to release the missile at the greatest possible speed at an optimum angle slightly below 45 deg. from a circle 7 ft in diameter, so that it lands within the prescribed throwing area.

Hammer speed and a rotational pattern are established during (usually two) preliminary swings before the hammer's speed is markedly increased and its plane of motion is steepened progressively during (usually three) turns (Fig. 180 shows only the second and third of these, with a delivery.)

The system of man and hammer rotates about an axis passing through a   a1   b   c   c1

d   d1   e   f

g   h   i1

j   j1   k   l   l1   *Figure 180*

Figure 181

the thrower's contact with the ground (Fig. 85). The good thrower works his way across the circle diameter by pivoting alternately on the heel and ball of his left foot (Fig. 180*a–h*) (right-handed thrower). Thus, in the course of making these turns, he moves the common axis from the rear to the front of the circle. Finally, he imparts even greater speed to the hammer-head by lifting it powerfully with his legs and trunk (Fig. 180 *i–l*).

As, in any rotation, a hammer's linear speed will be directly proportional to its distance from the common axis (see pages 72 and 85), in good throwing relaxed arms are used merely as a prolongation of the wire shaft, fully extended in the turns and final delivery—pulled out by centrifugal force (Fig. 180). Its range can also be improved by exerting a centripetal force on it through a *shifting backwards of the hips* (Fig. 181*a*) as distinct from leaning the upper body—which shortens the hammer's radius (Fig. 181*b*).

From Newton's First Law (see page 25) it follows that the hammer would move in a straight path but for the force of gravity and a centripetal (i.e. pulling-in) force exerted by the athlete—a force proportional to the square of the missile's linear speed. If, for example, the hammer's speed is doubled, the thrower must then exert four times the centripetal force, automatically increasing an equal but opposite centrifugal (i.e. pulling-out) force. The centrifugal force of the thrower on one side of the axis is the centripetal force causing the hammer to rotate on the other side.

Figure 182

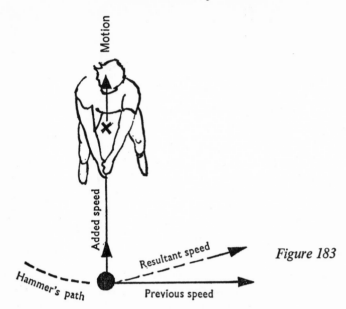

Figure 183

The athlete accelerates the hammer by exerting horizontal and vertical components of force.

(1) *Horizontally,* he is able to apply force only because of the friction between his feet and the ground—through the reactions of the ground to the forces exerted by his feet. This friction also enables the thrower to accelerate the hammer in this plane by either a linear or flail-like (i.e. circular) movement of the common axis (e.g. the rotational acceleration of a conker on a string in this plane is made possible by virtue of moving such an axis, Fig. 182).

Fig. 183 shows how the speed of the hammer-head can be increased horizontally as a result of the thrower's exerting a centripetal force; as, in good throwing, the arms are extended throughout, such a force can be applied only by moving the common axis (Fig. 183). In fact, its movement across the circle is essential to imparting the greatest possible centripetal impulse to the hammer-head, and to this end the weight of the thrower must be maintained over his pivoting leg throughout (for if this axis falls between the feet or over the trailing foot, progression across the circle is impaired).

Tangential acceleration is further improved when the thrower leads the hammer-head (Fig. 184). Here he obtains 'body torque' through

212

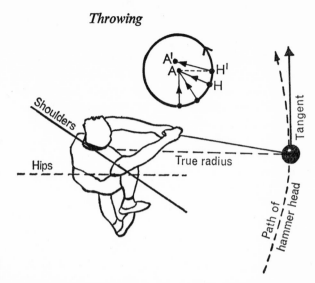

Figure 184

A plan view of a turning hammer thrower. When the *apparent* radius (i.e. a straight line from the thrower's left shoulder to the hammer-head) is at an angle to the true radius, the missile's speed is increased.

When the hammer's axis is moved from A to A', the direction of pull is changed to A'H' and now contains a horizontal component of force in the direction of the missile's motion.

leading markedly with his hips and legs, moving his feet 'fast and early' (Cullum*) in the turns. For by this means the thrower continuously moves the hammer's centre of motion *horizontally*, and in a direction parallel to that of the missile itself, urging the hammer forward while it continues to travel in a curved (though not circular) path. The play of the hips 'against' the shoulders fluctuates during a complete turn but whenever the wire shaft is not at right angles to the curve along which the hammer-head is moving (Fig. 184), the hammer will be accelerating and, correctly, the thrower will be 'maintaining contact' through his left arm (Cullum). (Note the reference to 'leading' the hammer-head here, as opposed to 'trailing' it. The latter, to a hammer thrower, indicates a bending of the right arm with a resulting shortening of hammer radius; whereas, to 'lead' the hammer indicates a trunk twist—infinitely preferable).

To re-emphasise: such methods of accelerating the hammer horizontally are possible only by virtue of the friction between the thrower's

* D. N. J. Cullum, 'Hammer Throwing' (A.A.A. Advanced Course Lectures, Loughborough Summer Schools, England, 1956-60).

feet and the ground, and this can attain its greatest value when both feet are in contact with the ground and the hammer-head is below the level of the shoulders. (Maximum friction, here, depends on the pressure between the feet and the ground (see page 58).)

This is particularly true of acceleration through 'body torque' (Fig. 184). In that phase of a turn where the thrower pivots on one foot (Fig. 180a), and with only its outside edge touching the ground, horizontal acceleration can therefore be only very small if, indeed, it is at all possible; for in such a position pressure between foot and ground has a minimum value.

(2) *Vertically*, the hammer can be accelerated upwards and downwards during each successive 360 deg. turn, and in good throwing this vertical acceleration increases progressively from turn to turn—and is of vital importance to the delivery (Fig. 180h–k).

(i) *Vertically upwards*. The hammer can be accelerated upwards as soon as the hammer-wire is inclined upwards to the vertical, and this acceleration would appear to attain its maximum value shortly after the hammer-head has passed its lowest point, i.e. off the right foot (right-handed athlete) (Figs. 36 and 180d1). Here, the force applied to the hammer-head is limited by that which the athlete can exert downwards through his feet (preferably both feet simultaneously) against the ground. Therefore, given the position from which to apply such a force, the limiting factor is the *strength* and speed of the athlete.

The direction of the reaction obtained from the ground will be upward with the hammer at its lowest point and will diminish gradually and change more to the horizontal as the hammer-head rises.

(ii) *Vertically downward*, acceleration is achieved by permitting the body weight to drop just before the hammer-head itself drops in its swings or turns. Here, therefore, the limiting factor to acceleration is

First turn   Third turn

Figure 185   a   b

the thrower's *weight*—which can be lowered with or without contact with the ground.

Fig. 185 illustrates how, with a steepening of the plane of hammer movement and a progressive increase in its linear speed from turn to turn, vertical means of acceleration become increasingly important and horizontal means comparatively less so.

Throwers often jump round on the last turn because the speed of the hammer is too great for their ability to advance their hips and feet in any other way or because they are off balance. However, by this means the hips are never so well advanced—relative to the shoulders and hammer-head—as in a suitably fast pivot on one foot; but for this, of course, the thrower needs tremendous speed and dexterity.

Figure 186

A final acceleration of the hammer can be achieved by simultaneously (a) *lifting* it into orbit while (b) exerting a centripetal force so as to *reduce its radius of motion*; for, assuming no change in the missile's angular momentum (the product of MVR), a reduction in R must be accompanied by an increase in V.* (Payne† has estimated a 2 per cent increase in tangential velocity through as little as a 2 inch shortening of the hammer's radius.)

From a position where knees and hips are well flexed, and with the athlete 'leading' the hammer-head (Fig. 180*i*), both legs—and particularly the left leg—drive vertically and the head and trunk are arched back (Fig. 180 *j–k*).

This violent change of posture not only lifts the hammer but, by raising the line of action of the athlete's centrifugal force about the feet, also causes a loss of balance away from the missile (Fig. 180*k*); but for this to increase the hammer's speed and to be as *prolonged* as possible, the thrower must increase his own angular velocity about the common axis; by accentuating the thrust from his left leg, he must make a

---

* Because the hammer-athlete system is not isolated from external forces, in fact there can only be a *tendency* towards the conservation of angular momentum.

† H. Payne, *Hammer Throwing*. (Amateur Athletic Association. England, 1969), page 61.

conscious effort to accelerate his trunk and head around his left foot (Fig. 186) so as *continually* to shorten the missile's radius about an axis passing through that foot and a point somewhere between his arms (Fig. 180*j–k*).

Discus. If a discus is to be thrown a maximum distance it must be released with the greatest possible speed at an optimum angle—the latter being influenced quite considerably by the aerodynamic factors discussed already (see page 200).

In the sense that both are rotational in character, some similarity exists between this event and hammer throwing. Yet, otherwise, they have little in common. For whereas the hammer is slung from a wire which can only transmit force along the direction in which the wire lies, the discus is thrown from an arm, and whenever the thrower's hand has a firm grasp on the implement there is little limitation to the direction in which that hand can exert force on the discus.

From a position at the rear of the 8 ft 2½ in. (2½ m) circle, and with his back to the direction of throw, the athlete executes several (usually no more than three) preliminary swinging movements, using his entire body—not the arm alone. These movements help to prepare him emotionally for the throw and develop a movement pattern important to the efficiency of the turning and throwing movements which follow.

The thrower then shifts his weight over his left (pivoting) foot, turns and drives quickly across the circle (Fig. 187*a–e*). Here, it is important to use just the correct quantity of spin on this pivoting foot; novices often spin too far, to the detriment of their throwing position, subsequently. In driving across the circle it is also important to maintain a correct relationship between this pivoting foot and the thrower's Centre of Gravity; the faster the movement across, the farther forward of this foot should be the Centre of Gravity. Through failure to maintain this relationship novice throwers often lose balance falling backwards in the throw. (Ryan.*) (See also pages 61, 62, 66 and 67.)

In this phase (Fig. 187*a–e*) the expert's shoulders turn through approximately 450 deg. and, correctly, he develops maximum controlled angular and linear velocities. In the turn—part pivot, part jump, part running movement—the axis of movement passes through his base —i.e. first his left foot (Fig. 187*b–c*) and then the right (Fig. 187*e*) (see also page 77). A relaxed throwing arm trails fairly wide of the body, encouraging maximum possible speed of movement in the throw

* F. Ryan, 'The discus turn and throw' (*Scholastic Coach*, 33, West 42nd Street. New York 36, U.S.A., March 1950), page 13.

which follows; for, for a given angular velocity, the linear speed of the discus will be proportional to its distance from the common axis. (See pages 71 and 85.)

The trailing of the throwing arm also increases the moment of inertia of the upper body relative to the common axis, tending to slow those parts of the body down in their rotation; simultaneously, by keeping the thighs close together in the turn (i.e. reducing their moment of inertia about this axis) the rotation of the lower parts can be speeded up. Hence, body torque (as important here as in hammer throwing) can be built up. However, some great throwers build up angular momentum in their hips and legs through a wide leg-sweep during the first half of the turn. When, subsequently, the free leg is pulled in, torque between hips and shoulders is increased—an effect enhanced by a deliberate effort to hold back the upper body by bending the free arm across the chest.

The expert discus thrower also advances his hips and feet relative to his upper body by stressing the pick-up and rotational movement of his free (right) leg as he drives from the rear of the circle, by getting his right foot to the ground again quickly and by positioning his front (left) foot without delay (Fig. 187*d–f*). And this is achieved without raising his Centre of Gravity unduly, and with both feet off the ground for only an instant—otherwise, when the thrower lands in the front half of the circle, his upper body will have begun to catch up his hips, to the detriment of body torque and the power of his throwing position.

The expert also lands on a flexed right leg and with his weight well over it (Fig. 187*e*). He then adds to the speed of the discus by transferring that weight from rear to front foot, thus shifting the common axis; simultaneously, he stretches and lifts powerfully with legs and trunk and unwinds his upper body and throwing arm through approximately 180 deg. of additional shoulder rotation (Fig. 187*f–i*). All this takes place against a bracing and lifting action of his left leg, the foot of which is placed only slightly to the side of his general line of direction across the circle (Fig. 187*g–h*); ideally this foot remains in contact with the ground until the discus has left the hand. (See pages 189–93.)

After the left foot meets the ground and the actual throwing movement begins (Fig. 187*f*) the path of the discus describes a spiral curve, first descending and then rising steeply, but inclining more to the horizontal as the point of release (just in front of the line of the shoulders) is approached. Early in its rise the hand has a firm grasp and during this period can exert a vertical or near-vertical force on

d   c   b   a

g   e

j   l   h   *Figure 187*

the implement. In fact, the lifting of the trunk and legs must take place at this time, while the hand can transmit vertical force.

Later, the upper edge of the discus drops away from the wrist and any force applied through the fingers must then pass through the Centre of Gravity of the implement—otherwise it will wobble, to the detriment of its stability in flight. Consequently a series of velocities is given to the discus at this stage, beginning vertically but tending towards the horizontal. A combination of these velocities results in the discus starting its flight with a negative angle of incidence. (See page 206.)

Shot. The technique of shot putting is simpler than that of each of the other three throwing events, lending itself easily to mechanical analysis through the use of ciné film.

By taking ciné pictures from a fixed camera set on a continuation of the line dividing the circle into front and rear halves, preferably against accurately-positioned background markings, and focused on a point approximately 3 ft directly above the middle of the circle, these pictures can be projected, subsequently, frame by frame or at other regular intervals of time, and the path of the shot can be plotted.

Then, provided the camera speed is known, it is possible to calculate the (*a*) time taken for the put, (*b*) acceleration of the shot in a sagittal plane, from stage to stage, (*c*) its path across the circle in this plane, (*d*) release speed, (*e*) height of the point of release, (*f*) and angle of projection; and from (*d*) (*e*) and (*f*) compute (*g*), the distance of the put.

Fig. 188 illustrates just such an analysis of a put by Arthur Rowe, Great Britain (former European record-holder), in 1958, where the missile was released (at a point marked by a cross (Fig. 188) 6 ft 6 in. above the ground, at an angle of 41 deg. and at a speed of 41 ft per second—which (allowing for a point of release 9 in. beyond the inside of the stop-board) gives a distance of 59 ft 5 in.

The diagram also illustrates the comparatively straight path of the shot from the rear of the circle to the point of release, with fewer undulations and less of a tendency to dip markedly in the middle of the circle than one often sees—proof that all Rowe's various body forces in this plane were acting in the most favourable direction. In this put the athlete applied his forces over a range of over 8 ft (as against the 7 ft of the circle's diameter).

A study of the dots marking the passage of the shot shows that by far the greatest accelerations occurred as the large forces of the legs and trunk were brought into play approximately half-way across the

Point of release ✕

Figure 188

circle, where the distance between the dots increases suddenly and considerably (Fig. 188). A more detailed analysis than is shown here also revealed that the shot's acceleration dropped as the arm thrust, but increased again when the athlete added a final wrist-snap as the shot rolled off his fingers.

The purpose of the glide (Fig. 189*b–d*) is primarily to give the athlete and the shot horizontal speed prior to the delivery in the front half of the circle. The glide is important, yet not too much importance should be attached to it, as it accounts for no more than 10 per cent of the total distance. Certainly, the glide ought never to be executed to the detriment of power of position and control in the delivery, subsequently; i.e. it should never take up too much of the circle, so cramping the putter's delivery; or be too fast, to the point of exceeding his 'critical' speed.

It can be seen that Rowe's glide (Fig. 188) took him rather less than half-way across the circle, permitting a breadth of base suited to his height, horizontal speed and lean over his rear leg.

The actual putting action must begin immediately the athlete's rear (right) foot comes to rest at the end of the glide, otherwise valuable time will elapse without acceleration being given to the shot. (See pages 189–91.) As soon as this rear foot lands, its leg can exert an efficient upward thrust and the trunk and shot can be raised.

However, since maximum body force and maximum rotation of the trunk about its long axis are possible only with the other foot used as

220

Figure 189

a point of resistance, the front foot should land only fractionally after the rear foot; here, there should be just sufficient rocking motion from one foot to the other to help keep the common Centre of Gravity moving forward. A slight rock will, in fact, help bring the front foot to the ground; on the other hand, with too much weight over the back leg at this stage, and with the front foot poised long in the air, the athlete will lose much, if not all, the speed built up during the glide.

Contrary to the view that the putting action 'is a movement which begins in the toes and ends in the fingers', in fact (as in almost all athletic activities) movement begins in the stronger but slower muscles surrounding the athlete's Centre of Gravity and is then taken up, below the hips, at the knees, ankles and feet, in that order; simultaneously, above the hips, it extends upwards through the putting shoulder, elbow, wrist and fingers. In its summation of forces (see pages 38 and 188), therefore, a technically sound putting action can be likened to the

221

throwing of a stone into a pool of water—causing the ripples to flow outward.

Theoretically, there can be no doubt that, throughout the putting movements in the front of the circle, the front foot should be firmly in contact with the ground, providing the necessary resistance for the hand to exert maximum force both vertically and horizontally. The vertical component of force must exceed the force of gravity to ensure continuous, though varying, upward acceleration. Horizontally, as soon as the hand rises above the centre of percussion the backward thrust of the shot on the hand encourages the front foot to move forward (see pages 191-4).

However, it must be admitted that a majority—if not all—of the world's best shot putters *do* in fact break contact with this front foot fractionally before the missile leaves the hand. This may be to avoid moving beyond the stop-board; for by this means, the athlete reduces some of his forward momentum. Or, the legs may be driving too vertically (possibly because the feet are too close together) or the arm striking too horizontally. Again, this could happen because of the accelerations developed by the legs and trunk—accelerations which may be too great for the strength of the arm; arm action may have to be delayed until these have been reduced, if not completed (see page 192).

Javelin. The ideal, in this event, is to combine maximum controlled approach-speed with a throwing position which enables maximum force to be applied to the javelin over the greatest possible range (see page 188), releasing it at an optimum angle (see pages 207-9). Throwers are rarely satisfied with their combining of these two largely ir-reconcilable factors; yet, always, their aim is to obtain an effective throwing position with the javelin already moving fast—and then, with the throwing shoulder travelling at maximum speed relative to the ground, to impart maximum hand speed in relation to the shoulder.

For the greater part of his 14-17 stride (overall) run-up the expert thrower holds the javelin over his shoulder in a position which permits relaxed, balanced running, and accelerates gradually into a horizontal speed governed by his ability to exert full body force, subsequently, in his throwing movements. Approach speed should depend upon body speed and strength (see page 189).

After 10-12 of these running strides he withdraws and aligns the javelin in preparation for the throw, turning and gradually leaning his trunk to the rear to adopt a powerful pulling position (Fig. 190a). The change in the angle of the trunk is particularly marked during the so-a   b   c

d   e   f

g   h   i   *Figure 190*

called 'cross-step' immediately prior to the throwing stride (Fig. 190*a–b*), where it is essential that the thrower contacts the ground with his right foot (right-handed athlete) before his body weight moves over and beyond this foot.

Here, in a good throw, the athlete's grip will be approximately 4 ft

223

behind his Centre of Gravity which, in turn, will be to the rear of his right foot (Fig. 190*b*) The line of the leading leg and trunk at this instant will be about 25 deg. to the vertical, but the angle should depend upon the speed of the run-up, the greater speed requiring a greater angle, and vice versa. The thrower coasts through this transition from running to throwing position, yet his strides quicken progressively.

Basically the javelin throwing action can be described as, first, a powerful pull exerted on the missile, followed by a lifting motion, where 'the thrower attempts to run off and away from the rear leg against the resistance of the front leg' (Pugh*) (Fig. 190*b–h*). Beginning as the right foot contacts the ground at the end of the cross-step and with the throwing arm comparatively straight and relaxed, a *pull from the shoulder* is applied as the weight of the body moves forward and the front foot reaches out (Fig. 190*c–d*). And as this weight moves ahead of the supporting foot, the right leg drives hard to add to this pulling movement and keep the right hip, in particular, moving fast into the throw. In good throwing, this transference of weight against the resistance of the front leg occurs without a premature turning of the shoulders to the front; in fact, the hips twist fractionally ahead of the shoulders.

So widespread are the feet in good javelin throwing that the rear leg completes its drive before the front foot contacts the ground (Fig. 190*d*). Trunk rotation occurs mainly by virtue of the front foot's resistance to horizontal motion. A quick turning-in of the rear knee and foot adds to hip speed and coincides with an outward rotation and raising of the throwing elbow which are essential to final flail-like arm action.

If the trunk is too erect and the throwing base too narrow for the athlete's approach speed, he will lack sufficient range over which to apply his body forces and will tend quickly to rotate in a sagittal plane over and beyond his front foot in delivery, pulling the javelin down (Fig. 191*a*). On the other hand, if he leans back too far and his feet are too widespread, the Centre of Gravity's forward speed will be reduced excessively (see pages 191–5), the hips will not pass over the forward foot and, incorrectly, the trunk will pivot about the hips, shortening the radius of movement in a sagittal plane and, again, pulling the javelin down in delivery (Fig. 191*b*).

It is difficult to estimate the actual loss in forward speed of the Centre of Gravity due to the impact of the front foot with the ground, but even

---

* D. L. Pugh, *Javelin Throwing* (Amateur Athletic Association, England, 1960), page 19.

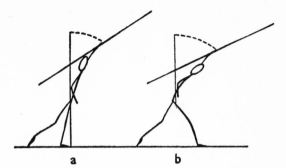

Figure 191

a   b

in a good throw it seems likely that this will be about one quarter of its original horizontal speed, depending upon the efficiency with which the front foot takes up the shock on impact (see pages 91 and 193). However, it may well be that the throwing shoulder at least maintains, if not increases, its linear speed, because of its distance above the Centre of Gravity.

(M. J. Ellis and H. H. Lockwood agree* that the speed of the throwing shoulder increases markedly as the front foot meets the ground, but suggest that this is due to the shoulder's rapid rotation about the body's longitudinal axis. In analysing film of one thrower they found that his Centre of Gravity did not describe an arc during the throwing stride, because of his flexed front leg, which kept the Centre of Gravity moving horizontally. They concluded that the hinged effect in this event occurs more in a *transverse* than sagittal plane, commenting, 'Perhaps, whilst the hinged moment effect (in a sagittal plane) is theoretically and mechanically ideal, the stresses that it would place on the thrower are such that the innate protective mechanisms of the body would not allow it to be used, even assuming that the thrower is strong enough to remain rigid.') In all probability the most valuable effect in the checking of forward motion lies in the 'bowing' of the body— a movement which rapidly stretches the trunk's flexor muscles, invoking powerful eccentric contractions.

Because, in good throwing, the athlete's rear foot must break effective contact with the ground before the arm applies its forces, *the arm's* first *pulling movement*, acting at shoulder-level below the point of percussion, must be exerted against the inertia of the thrower's body,

* M. J. Ellis and H. H. Lockwood. 'Javelin Throw, John McSorley.' (*A.A.A. Coaching Newsletter* No. 26, January-April 1964; Amateur Athletic Association, England), page 6.

so reducing his forward speed. However, once the front foot meets the ground (Fig. 190*e*) it remains in contact until the javelin is released, and so provides an essential resistance not only to any vertical compon-

Figure 192

ent of the force of the arm action, but also to those horizontal components exerted, subsequently, above the point of percussion (see pages 189–94).

The final flail-like arm action of the good javelin thrower is brought about, first, by outwardly rotating the elbow (Fig. 190) and raising it higher than the hand grasping the javelin—'leaving that hand behind' (Pugh*)—before quickly extending the forearm and hand to apply further force vertically and through the javelin's length.

Fig. 192 illustrates the range of movement at the elbow, and Fig. 193 gives a diagrammatic interpretation of this flailing arm action. SEH approximates the position of the throwing arm during the earlier phases of throwing movement, while SE1H1 is the result of an extremely fast action of the upper-arm, SE1. SE2H2 represents the arm's position

Figure 193

at the instant of delivery, where the outward rotation of the elbow permits greater extension than that shown in Fig. 192.

This flailing arm action is superior to a straight-arm, bowling action, because:

* Ibid., page 15.

(i) the muscles acting between the forearm and upper arm, as well as the muscles acting between the shoulder and upper arm, can be used to produce force;

(ii) the small moment of inertia of the comparatively light forearm and hand about the elbow joint does not hinder greater angular speed of the forearm relative to the elbow (although, of course, the moment of inertia of the javelin about this joint must also be considered); and

(iii)) In a straight-arm rotation about the shoulder, angular speed would have to be developed against the considerable moment of inertia of the whole arm and javelin.

Thus the essential *pulling* character of a good javelin throw derives from (*a*) the motion of the body in front of the missile, (*b*) the body's rotation in two planes—sagittal and transverse, and (*c*) a final flail-like arm action. This pulling movement can take place over as much as 14 ft (Pugh*)—from the moment the right foot lands at the end of the cross-step (Fig. 190*b*) to the instant of release (midway between Fig. 190*g–h*), producing release speeds in excess of 60 m.p.h.

* Ibid., page 11.

Appendix

Many aspects of rotational movement important to athletics (much of it involving the conservation of angular momentum) can be demonstrated on a turntable, preferably with a stool attachment. Some demonstrations also require a weighted cycle wheel.

These experiments have to be confined to movement in a horizontal plane, for a turntable can react only to movement in that plane; but the principles illustrated apply to motion in any plane.

Figure 1

A turntable (1) should be level and stable and as frictionless as possible; of sufficient size to support a variety of positions, yet with the smallest possible moment of inertia. It should include levelling devices—adjustable legs with, ideally, spirit levels. A built-in friction control is recommended, as even a marginally-tilted smooth-running turntable will make demonstrating difficult. A straight line painted across the axis can be a useful guide, in some experiments, as to the extent of rotation.

The cycle wheel (2) should be equipped with two detachable handles which allow the hub to revolve independently. To increase the wheel's moment of inertia (and, therefore, its turning effect on the platform), its rim should be weighted until the whole weighs 8–10 lb.

Figure 2

Appendix

Series A **The effect of a change in 'I' on angular velocity**

1	**2**	**3**

1 Two light shots are held with arms outstretched and the turntable system is then rotated.
2 Its angular velocity is

3 markedly increased when the arms and weights are drawn in close to the chest; but the total angular momentum of the system remains constant.

Series B **Transference of angular momentum from a part to the whole**

1	**2**	**3**	**4**

1 The wheel is spun and
2 then, rotating horizontally, is given to the person on the turntable.

3 First kept clear of the body, it
4 is then checked against the chest, transferring its angular momentum to the system as a whole.

Series C **Transference of angular momentum, with emphasis on its directional quality**

1   **2**   **3**

1 The wheel, spinning in a horizontal plane, is given to the person on the turntable.
2 Thus, the turntable system's total angular momentum is concentrated in the wheel.

3 When the latter is turned to spin vertically, its earlier angular momentum in a horizontal plane, conserved in the system, now turns the table in the same sense. (Since the table cannot react to the wheel's new rotation, the earth absorbs this new reaction.)

Series D **Action and reaction**

1   **2**   **3**

1 The wheel, rotating in a vertical plane, is given to the person on the turntable.
2 When the wheel is turned horizontally, the turntable system (of which the wheel is a part) rotates with equal angular momentum but in an opposite direction.
3 When the first position is resumed the turntable stops.

Appendix

Series E 'Taking up' angular momentum

1   **2**   **3**

1 The spinning wheel, rotating in a vertical plane, is given to the person on the turntable and
2 the system is then rotated.

3 When the wheel is turned horizontally to rotate in the same sense as the turntable, it absorbs (i.e. takes up) a quantity of the table's original angular momentum—the amount depending upon the angular momenta imparted to wheel and turntable initially.
a With the wheel's angular momentum less than that of the table, the latter will continue to rotate, but more slowly.
b When the wheel's angular momentum is equal to that of the table, the turntable stops (as shown here).
c When the wheel's angular momentum exceeds that of the table, the latter reverses its rotational direction (thus conserving the system's total angular momentum).

231

Bibliography

ADAMSON, G. T., 'Some Facts and Fallacies on Fitness Training', A.A.A. *Coaching Newsletter* No. 15, July 1960, Amateur Athletic Association.

ALFORD, J. W. L., 'Sprinting and Relay Racing', Amateur Athletic Association, 1959.

——, 'Middle Distance Running and Steeplechasing', Amateur Athletic Association, 1960.

ARISTOTLE, 'On the Gait of Animals', Vol. II, Book 9, *Great Books of the Western World*, Encyclopaedia Britannica Inc., 1952.

BALL, A. F., 'The Mechanics of Diving', unpublished thesis, Loughborough College of Education.

BARRETT, L., 'The Universe and Dr. Einstein', New American Library Inc., New York 22; 1962.

BUNN, J. W., *Scientific Principles of Coaching*, Prentice-Hall, Englewood Cliffs, N. J., U.S.A.,

COOPER, L., DALZELL, D. and SILVERMAN, E., *Flight of the Discus*, Division of Engineering Science, Purdue University, Indiana, U.S.A., May 1959.

COUNSILMAN, JAMES E., *The Science of Swimming*, Prentice-Hall, 1968.

CULLUM, D. N. J., 'Hammer Throwing', A.A.A. Advanced Course Lectures, Loughborough Summer Schools, 1956–60.

DOHERTY, K., *Modern Track and Field*, Prentice-Hall, 1953.

DYATCHKOV, V. M., *High Jumping*, Moscow, 1966.

DYSON, G. H. G., *Body-mechanics without tears*, A.G.M., Mathematical Association, 1956.

——, 'Elevation and Rotation', Royal Academy of Dancing *Gazette*, September 1955 (R.A.D.).

——, *High Jumping*, Amateur Athletic Association, 4th edition, 1959.

EGGLETON, M. GRACE, *Muscular Exercise*, Kegan Paul, Trench, Trubner and Co., Ltd., 1936.

ENG YOON TAN, 'Research into the Hop, Step and Jump', National Collegiate Track Coaches Association, 29th Annual Meeting. Published by 'Champions on Film', 303½ SO Main Street, Ann Arbor, Michigan, U.S.A.

232

GANSLEN, R. V., 'Aerodynamic factors which influence discus flights', Research Report, College of Arts and Sciences, University of Arkansas, May 1958.

——, 'Finnish Javelin Throwing', *Scholastic Coach*, 33 West 22nd Street, New York 36, February 1950.

——, *The Mechanics of the Pole Vault*, John S. Swift and Coy., St. Louis, 4th edition 1959–60.

GRAY, JAMES, *How Animals Move*, Cambridge University Press, 1953.

GRIMSEHL, E., *A Textbook of Physics: Vol. I. Mechanics*, Blackie, 1932.

HAWLEY, G., *An Anatomical Analysis of Sports*, A. S. Barnes and Co., New York.

HILL. A. V., *Muscular Activity*, Williams and Wilkins, Baltimore, 1925.

HOPPER, B. J., 'Rotation—a vital factor in Athletic Technique', Track Technique, Nos. 9–17. *Track and Field News*.

——, *Notes on the dynamical basis of physical movement'*, St. Mary's College, Twickenham, London.

HOUSDEN, E, F., 'Mechanics applied to Discus Throwing', *Discobolus*, The Discus Circle Magazine, issue no. 8, December 1959.

——, 'An analysis of the effects of the acceleration of the free leg in various athletic events', *Coaching Review*, March 1966, Royal Canadian Legion.

KARPOVICH, P. V., *Physiology of Muscular Activity*, Saunders, 1953.

KUZNETSOV, V. L., 'Mastery of Javelin Throwing Technique', Track Technique No. 2, December 1960, *Track and Field News*.

LINDHARD, J. *Theory of Gymnastics*, Methuen, 2nd edition 1939.

MCINTOSH, P., and HAYLEY, H. W. B., 'An investigation into the running long jump', *Journal of Physical Education*, November 1952.

MOREHOUSE, L. E., and COOPER, J. M., *Kinesiology*, Henry Kimpton, 1950.

MUIR, J., *Of Men and Numbers*, Dell Publishing Company, New York 17, 1962.

PAYNE, HOWARD, *Hammer Throwing*, Amateur Athletic Association, England, 1969.

PEARSON, G. F. D., *Athletics*, Thomas Nelson & Sons Ltd., 1963.

PHARAOH, M., 'Observations on Discus Throwing', A.A.A. *Coaching Newsletter* No. 4, April 1957, Amateur Athletic Association.

PUGH, D. L., *Javelin Throwing*, Amateur Athletic Association, 1960.

RASCH, P. J., and BURKE, R. K., *Kinesiology and Applied Anatomy*, Henry Kimpton.

ROGERS, E. M., *Physics for the Inquiring Mind*, Princeton University Press, 1962.

RYAN, F., 'The discus turn and throw', *Scholastic Coach*, 33 West 42nd Street, New York 36, March 1950.

SCHUPPE, HANS, *Physik der Leibesübungen*, Ferdinand Enke Verlag, Stuttgart.

SIMONS, J. C., 'An introduction to surface-free behaviour', *Ergonomics*, Vol. VII, January 1964.

STEINHAUS, A. H., 'The Physiology of Exercise', Series of lectures, Chicago 1948.

STUKELEY, W. *Memoirs of Newton's Life*, Taylor and Francis, 1936. (From a manuscript now preserved by the Royal Society, London.)

TARRANT, G. T. P., 'Mechanics of human and animal activity', *School Science Review*, No 78, December 1938.

WEBB, P., *Bioastronautics Data Book*, Webb Associates, Yellow Springs, Ohio, 1964.

WELLS, K. F., *Kinesiology*, Saunders, 1950.

WILLIAMS, M. and LISSNER, H. R., *Biomechanics of Human Motion*, W. B. Saunders Coy., 1962.

WILT, F., 'Run, Run, Run', *Track and Field News Inc.*, 1965.

Index

235

Index

Index

Index